THE BEST FILM I NEVER MADE

Bruce Beresford lives in Sydney. He has directed more than thirty films and numerous operas, and is the author of *Josh Hartnett Definitely Wants to Do This* (2007). He is filming an adaptation of Madeleine St John's novel *The Women in Black*. *The Best Film I Never Made* collects the best of Bruce's occasional writings from the past fifteen years.

bruceberesford.org

The Best Film I Never Made

AND OTHER STORIES ABOUT A LIFE IN THE ARTS

BRUCE BERESFORD

TEXT PUBLISHING MELBOURNE AUSTRALIA

Earlier versions of some of the pieces in this book appeared in various newspapers, magazines, catalogues and edited collections.

textpublishing.com.au

The Text Publishing Company
Swann House
22 William Street
Melbourne Victoria 3000
Australia

First published in 2017 by The Text Publishing Company

Book design by Jessica Horrocks
Cover photo (c. 1980) © David Montgomery/Getty Images
Back cover photo (2017) © Rafy
Typeset by J&M Typesetting

Printed and bound in Australia by Griffin Press, an Accredited ISO AS/NZS 14001:2004 Environmental Management System printer

National Library of Australia Cataloguing-in-Publication entry
ISBN: 9781925603101 (paperback)
ISBN: 9781925626032 (ebook)
Creator: Beresford, Bruce, 1940– author.
Title: The best film I never made: and other stories about a life in the arts / by Bruce Beresford.
Subjects: Beresford, Bruce, 1940–. Motion picture producers and directors—Australia—Anecdotes. Motion picture industry. Motion pictures—Production and direction—Biography. Motion pictures—Australia—Production and direction—Anecdotes.

This book is printed on paper certified against the Forest Stewardship Council® Standards. Griffin Press holds FSC chain-of-custody certification SGS-COC-005088. FSC promotes environmentally responsible, socially beneficial and economically viable management of the world's forests.

Contents

III
Behind the Screen

IV
Opera, Painters, Writers

I

Family, Journeys, Memories

Family Tree

He insisted he stay on in the house in the country after our mother died. 'You'll never get him out,' friends said to me. 'They never want to let go, even though they'd be much better off in a retirement home.' This was, sadly, true, even though my sister and I visited a number of places and then took him the brochures, along with improbable stories of the wonderful time he was going to have with all the other old people.

We weren't being entirely selfish. He did very little work around the house or large garden when our energetic mother was alive and I saw no reason for an onslaught of activity. I doubted if he was capable of cooking anything at all. When I was a child, on the rare occasions our mother was away for a few days, he fed my sister and me on chips. Cut very thick. Cooked in lashings of oil. For every meal. I recall being delighted at the time.

'What will you do all day?' my sister demanded. He spluttered and rambled, trotting out his usual array of unfinished sentences, though the tone was unmistakable—no pioneer home. I knew what he'd do all day. Just as he'd always done, but more of it. If there was no cricket or AFL on the television, an amble across to the general store, down to the tourist souvenir shop and/or up the hill to the pub (now smartened up and run by a couple of young men from Paddington), where he would bore anyone he could find with half-remembered and incoherently presented stories of his life as a travelling washing-machine salesman in the 1930s.

True, there were a few local friends but I suspected they were more the friends of our mother and would now take evasive action. Perhaps there were already very few left. Most were reliant on Zimmer frames and were given to dying on the bowling green or while sipping cups of tea as a television newsreader described events in a world they had long ceased to understand.

The first time I visited after her death—it must have been a couple of months, as I'd been away working—I was amazed at the changes, even though I had foreseen them. The grass had grown up and either choked or hidden all my mother's flowers. The front door was jammed shut and there was glass all over the porch. It was dark and there was no light from anywhere in the house.

I walked around to the side of the house and pushed aside the pendulous passionfruit vine that hung over the kitchen door. I flicked the light switch with no result. The kitchen smelt and was filthy with empty baked-bean tins all over the floor and sink. (There were no dirty plates as he ate directly from the tins.) The living room had wet clothes strewn over the sofas and the moonlight revealed large mushrooms growing on the carpet. Newspapers were piled everywhere, hundreds of them. He'd hoarded them all his life, but my mother had succeeded in keeping them out of the house, apart from a pile in the bedroom, with the result that the garage was so full of them there was no possibility of using it for the car. The car, also, was full of newspapers.

The odd thing was that, although he bought newspapers every day, I could never recall him reading anything in them except the sports pages. There was no point in mentioning to him any catastrophe, revolution, political event, murder or robbery. He'd never heard of it. (He was evidently taken by complete surprise when he was called up for service at the beginning of the Second World War; he had no inkling of the approaching conflict or any clue as to the identity of the antagonists. The Australian army quickly realised that he would be a liability and sent him home. He spent the duration of the conflict, he explained to me, as a 'Sussex Street Commando'. Commando! Imagining him swimming up crocodile-infested tropical rivers with a knife between his teeth, I used to boast about this to my school friends, until I found out from a much-decorated uncle that it was an office job.) If any effort was made to remove any of the newspapers, even the pre-war ones, he resisted vigorously, proclaiming, 'There's an article in one of them I want to read.'

I found him in the living room, sitting in front of the television wearing an old bean-stained dressing gown, watching the cricket. 'G'day,' he said casually. 'Look at this...Richards...my godfather, he can hit. Look...he...like Keith Miller. Remember when we saw Miller?...Lots of...'

I remembered. We'd seen Miller lots of times at the Sydney Cricket Ground. Being burnt to a crisp at the cricket ground, while the agonisingly slow games drifted on day after day, was the main thing we'd done together. He didn't show much interest in anything else, certainly not my schoolwork. I don't think he even found out I'd been to university, though his interest perked up when I became a film director. We even went to a few movies, though the plots and characters all baffled him as they'd become so much more complicated since the days of Errol Flynn and Ronald Colman. After their deaths his interest in movies lapsed.

I stayed with him a few days. I bought some light bulbs and opened all the windows to let in some air. He shut them all again. I found him showering fully dressed—except for his shoes—so that he could wash his clothes as well as his body. He said it saved time. I said he didn't need to save time and should use the washing machine. I couldn't even persuade him to hang the wet clothes outside. He continued to hang them over the sofa and was happy to wear them soggy.

I took him out shopping and for some meals in the local town down the mountain. He was angry because I wouldn't let him drive the car. He'd always been an appalling driver and as a result had faced numerous court cases. Over the years he had lost his licence a number of times, not that this prevented him from driving for even one day. On the bridge over the Hawkesbury River I pointed out to him the spot where he'd missed the bridge approach and gone straight into the river with my mother and aunt as passengers. They'd all been rescued, in the middle of the night, by some American tourists. He scoffed at this proof of his incompetence, just as he snorted and avoided my attempts at involving him in a discussion—as a prelude to reintroducing the subject of the retirement village—of the rundown house, the ridiculous diet (baked beans and ice cream), or even the fact he'd never changed a light bulb but was content to sit in the dark and then find his way from room to room with a torch.

A couple of smart little restaurants had opened, all cappuccino, goat cheese and focaccia. He walked past these, insisting on Kentucky Fried Chicken. I protested, but had to give in. Almost anything was better than the baked beans. Was I imagining it, or were people walking towards us suddenly crossing the street? He waved (he'd lived in the district for years and knew almost everyone) and called to them effusively, though they managed to scamper away, intent on appointments to right and left. Only one poor old lady on a Zimmer frame lacked the necessary speed and so was cornered and told about my career. How I had always been obsessed with films, et cetera, et cetera. He raved on and on to the poor old thing, skilfully blocking her feeble efforts to inch away from him. I doubt if she'd seen a film since the days of Shirley Temple and had no idea what this 'director' could possibly do. Didn't actors make up the stories?

As I lay in bed, in the damp sheets, I consoled myself with the thought that at least he didn't drink. Only an occasional beer. He could have been in this tumbledown house with baked beans and no lights in an alcoholic stupor. Then he could have fallen through the big picture window and rolled right down the mountain.

I phoned my sister and told her I couldn't even involve him in a conversation about moving, let along get his agreement. The visit depressed me, not really because of him, but for all the memories of my mother. I hunted through an old chest for some pictures of her. There were only two or three.

In one of them she was seventeen years old, her face unlined, her dark hair pulled back severely in the fashion of the time, her eyes sparkling with joy and youth and optimism.

...

I didn't see him again for over a year. I went to America to make a film. I called him a few days after arriving back in Sydney. I couldn't face the house again and suggested he come to the city and stay with me.

'You took the car keys with you,' he said, accusingly.

'It's not a good idea for you to drive. You can get the train down.'

'You come up here. There's someone I want you to meet.'

'Not if you're going to tell everyone we run across that I'm a film director.'

'Why are you going on about that again? What does it...'

'It embarrasses me.'

I thought I'd better face up to it and check out the house. Maybe I could arrange, again, for a gardener and cleaner. He'd sent the previous ones away, saying, despite overwhelming and clearly visible evidence to the contrary, that he had no problem maintaining the house or garden.

He asked me who was in the film I'd done. I named four famous actors but he'd never heard of any of them.

They were all post-Errol Flynn. He was impressed, though, that Hurd Hatfield had played a minor part. I'd never understood why, but he'd always been an admirer of *The Picture of Dorian Gray*, a 1945 film that had been Hurd's sole claim to fame. Was it Hatfield's good looks that impressed him? Did he imagine a resemblance? Old photographs showed my father as handsome and slim when young. I always thought, judging by the Errol Flynn moustache, that he saw himself as a movie-star type. He'd even worked as an extra in some obscure Australian films of the 1930s. No doubt his acting career suffered through the same lack of application that characterised everything he did.

Or did *Dorian Gray* appeal because it dealt with the transference of guilt to a painting of Dorian? I still remember the visits to various girlfriends when he was a commercial traveller (Bodega Wines succeeded the washing machines) and I, as a very small boy, would be left for hours sitting in a parked car outside city apartment buildings or suburban houses. I remember, too, the screaming matches and weeping apologies when my mother found out about some of these liaisons, no doubt because he showed no more skill at deceit and subterfuge than he did at anything else.

As I drove towards the mountains I compiled in my head a list of the bizarre rules he'd imposed in my childhood, all of them accepted at the time, most of them only questioned when I was in high school and came into contact with the families of school friends, causing me to query previously held tenets of 'normal' behaviour. Because he found the noise of footsteps irritating, we weren't allowed to wear shoes in the house; even visitors had to take them off at the front door. The radio was never to be switched on. At one point, and for some years, my sister and I had to be in our pyjamas at 4.30 p.m. and in bed by 6—humiliating for a ten-year-old whose friends were all out in the street playing cricket. All pets were banned as even a cat's padding paws kept him awake at night. He bought a rifle and shot neighbours' animals when they strayed into our yard, a pastime that did not endear me to the local kids. No one was allowed to speak at the dinner table, but had to point at anything that was wanted. Sundays were the worst. He wanted to 'have a little lie-in' and invariably did so until three in the afternoon. We were not allowed to get out of bed on this day until we heard him moving around the house.

I thought of my own children and how much easier their lives are. How hard I tried to make their childhoods more fun than mine had been. But...if one of them were writing this, how would I be portrayed? I've had hints from them, intercepted glances during conversations, that imply I am not the reasonable and amiable father I imagine myself to be.

He wouldn't tell me who he wanted me to meet but pushed me back out to the car almost immediately, clearly anxious to avoid any conversation about the further deterioration of the house, which now looked like the set for a Tennessee Williams play about white trash in the Deep South.

We drove back down the mountain, then along a dirt road that went for miles alongside the river, past old farmhouses and an occasional health farm or camping site. Finally, we went up a driveway towards an attractive double-storey brick farmhouse built in the mid-nineteenth century.

I was introduced to Herb Gillespie, a stocky man in his early sixties, weathered and brown from a life lived outdoors, though with a smooth face, devoid of life's experiences, as is often found among nuns or the intellectually disabled. As we shook hands in the kitchen he took off his hat to reveal an almost completely bald head. His eyes were unnaturally bright and of no real colour, just that of an empty lemonade bottle.

'Herb's got something to show you,' my father said, his voice assuming a reverential tone that puzzled me. He led the way into the living room, which had been furnished sometime in the 1920s and never altered since. I was admiring some of the pieces when my father indicated I should look at the wall. Herb gestured towards a large chart that was hanging there. I went closer. It was a genealogy chart of some sort, but one with far more rambling ramifications that the ones I remembered from school about the kings and queens of England.

'You see,' said my father, his voice tense with excitement, 'Herb is a direct descendant of Jesus Christ.'

'Oh...yes...of course,' I mumbled, glancing across at Herb, who smiled slightly at me in a self-deprecating kind of way, though his strange eyes seemed to have an extra glint. I thought it might be prudent to examine the chart with some pretence of interest. In silence, I spent some minutes studying the convoluted lines that led from Bethlehem to Herb Gillespie in Freemans Reach, Australia.

As we drove away there was a long silence, unusual for my father, who filled every second with prattle. Now he was waiting for me to tell him how stunned I was at the revelation. I couldn't help myself. 'What a load of crap,' I said.

'What do you mean? You saw the chart!'

'Anyone could make up a chart like that. You couldn't possibly take it seriously!'

'Why not? Why shouldn't Herb be descended from Jesus?'

I tried to think of an answer that was theologically irrefutable. I fossicked around among the remnants of my biblical knowledge, gained, but now mostly forgotten, while researching a dismal biblical movie.

'If he was, don't you think he'd be better known?' This was the best I could do. 'He'd be a celebrity if it was genuine, not a farmer in the Hawkesbury Valley!'

'He's just modest. He doesn't want people to know.'

I looked across at him. His lower jaw was thrust

forward in a way that told me discussion was pointless as well as tedious.

'You're just a cynic,' he murmured at me. 'You were always like that, even when you were a little boy. You never believe anyone.'

...

Apart from an AFL game we went to a couple of weeks later, I never saw him alive again. My sister called me in Los Angeles a year later to tell me he'd died after watching football on television. I was about to begin a film but arranged to delay it for a few days and flew back for the funeral. It was held at a small bush church, some miles from the nearest town. The day was extraordinarily windy. All the eucalypts groaned, creaked and rustled. I felt like an extra from an antipodean *Wuthering Heights*. Predictably, there were very few people present. Only my sister and her family and an old couple from the bowling club. Luckily, Herb Gillespie didn't show up, so I was spared any insights into the afterlife that his lineage might have provided.

A young and absurdly cheerful employee of the funeral director took me to see the body stretched out in an appropriately dimly lit room. 'Big bloke.' He grinned at me. 'I had a lot of trouble squeezing him into that suit.'

In fact, I'd never seen him look so smart. Suit, white shirt and tie. Alive, he always dressed in clothes bought from an opportunity shop—which, with their mixture of textures and colours, gave him the air of an old-time circus clown.

Two well-dressed elderly couples arrived just before the service. I noticed them and whispered to my sister, but she shook her head. After the brief and perfunctory rites, performed by a bad-tempered minister who was resenting time spent away from the golf course or other, possibly sinister, pursuits, I spoke to the late arrivals.

'Were you friends of my father?' I asked, not expecting an interesting answer.

'We're his sisters,' one of them said.

'His sisters! I didn't know he had any sisters.'

They had seen the death notice we had placed in the *Age* and flown up from Melbourne for the funeral of a brother who, I was told, had left home at nineteen, never to return or contact them again.

'But why would he have done that?'

'We don't know. He was such a nice boy. Very polite and very bright. Mum never got over it.'

My sister and I went through all his papers over the next week or so, not that there were many of them, thinking that we might find something relating to his background, his sudden departure from his family. There were a few poems written when he was in his twenties: quite good, I thought, for someone who had not shown the slightest interest in writing or reading anything other than *How to Win Friends and Influence People* (this failed) and *How to Stop Worrying and Start Living* (ditto). We learnt from the sisters that he had been very disturbed, as a teenager, by the sudden death of another sister, from one of those illnesses that killed in those days but are easily dealt with today. She had died literally in his arms, we were told.

People are too complicated and the influences on them too varied for me to think that the sister's death was the 'Rosebud' that explains my father's life, though I believe it affected him profoundly and permanently. He never mentioned it, and people rarely talk about those things that have had the most impact on them.

I still occasionally run into some of his old cronies, who invariably say, 'Oh, your dad! What a great bloke he was. So easygoing. Such a lot of fun…' I have never remembered him like that.

2004

My Parents

My parents are buried in St David's (which must be one of the smallest churches in Australia) churchyard as they lived almost opposite, at Kurrajong Heights, for some years. Both were seventy-nine when they died.

It has been said to me, by people who knew them locally, that they were particularly fun-loving. It's unfair to say there were no moments of hilarity, but I couldn't say that 'fun-loving' would describe either of them.

My mother was nicknamed Bubbles by her older friends and I think it referred to her bosom. She worked hard and ran the family electrical shop in Windsor (previously in Parramatta) for at least twenty years. I always noticed she was a dynamic, if eccentric, saleswoman who knew little about the products she was selling. I remember being amused as she enthused about a washing machine to a bewildered couple, although she had no idea how to turn it on.

Like my father, she had few interests. She was garden-obsessed (although the amount of hours invested in it were not reflected in the result), read the occasional romance novel and liked to bet small amounts of money on the horses. She had only a few close friends and was inclined to trade these in with regularity because of imagined slights.

She was born in Adelaide—of Norwegian descent on her mother's side, she alleged. Her stories about her past increased in invention in proportion to the ability of the listener to access the truth. I heard her tell people that she 'grew up in a large house with a private chapel', that she 'acted on stage with the Adelaide Shakespeare Company—and with Sir Robert Helpmann'. She left Adelaide at the age of nineteen in 1929 and I doubt if there was a Shakespeare company there at that time. When I met Robert Helpmann in the 1970s I told my mother, quite innocently, that I would mention her to him. She immediately became agitated and I realised the thespian claim was a fantasy.

At other times she claimed to have aristocratic English

ancestry (her father was in fact from the East End of London) and to have visited Paris a number of times (she never travelled overseas, except for one brief trip to Singapore). When I went to England in 1963 she gave me a document that was, she claimed, proof of the family's aristocratic lineage. She urged me to take it to a heraldic college for verification. With understandable hesitation, but under considerable pressure, I did so—and was told it was a well-known and widely circulated fake. Yet she must have convinced herself of the verisimilitude of the document, otherwise why put it to the test?

Both of my parents had little education, probably because both were from poor families. My mother was one of eight siblings and her father was a trick cyclist—not a profitable occupation. On my father's side my grandfather was a conductor on the trams in Melbourne. Schooldays were never discussed by either of my parents but I'm fairly certain both left school around the age of fourteen or fifteen. I don't recall either showing the remotest interest in my schooling, and my mother became strikingly unsure of herself when I was in my late teens and she met some of my friends either from university or the art world. She would affect an almost incomprehensible English accent and proclaim her love of art and ballet—two subjects of which she knew nothing.

My father had been born Frederic Leslie Swift. My sister and I only found that he had changed his name—to Leslie Beresford—when we discovered a document after he died. All efforts to discover the motivation behind the change have failed. There was a Beresford Street opposite the house where he grew up in Brunswick, a Melbourne suburb now being gentrified but of little distinction from at least 1910–90. Also, he was a great fan of an Errol Flynn film called *The Perfect Specimen*, in which Flynn's name was Beresford. There was certainly a resemblance to Flynn, revealed in photographs of his younger days, so perhaps this was enough to trigger the name change? Or did he at some time escape a love affair; was there a child born out of wedlock? Was he on the run for passing dud cheques? No evidence has been found to support these suggestions, which remain merely speculation.

He had been a salesman from the age of nineteen and was successful in the pre-war years, I have been told. He travelled the outback selling vacuum cleaners, washing machines and wine—not simultaneously, but in that order. Sometime in the 1950s he opened an electrical business in Parramatta and later moved it to Windsor. It was not a commercial success, largely, I always believed, because of his inability to put in an appearance before 2 p.m. He would wake about 10 a.m., then drift around the house pointlessly for hours in a dressing gown. When he dressed, his ensembles were invariably bizarre. In summer he would wear shorts with long white socks and a pith helmet on which was written 'Beresford's hat'. He looked like he had mislaid his safari. In the colder weather his apparel was more conventional. He favoured coats without lapels, a fashion he was convinced would be adopted worldwide. It has yet to catch on. At least he wore regular trousers. An odd touch was the absence of socks with his leather shoes. He claimed this was not uncomfortable. He was called up for the Second World War but proved a poor soldier and was sent home after a year.

When I was a child he was a remarkably silent character given to sudden and frightening outbursts of temper. He was chronically depressed and visited numerous psychiatrists over the years, so many, in fact, that by the late 1950s he was finding it difficult to engage one who was any longer willing to talk to him. A number of them tried to encourage him to acquire some interests, perhaps in the form of a pet or a hobby, though these schemes all failed. We acquired an occasional dog, though he invariably ended by hating the poor animal and then arranging its disappearance—to the chagrin of my sister and myself, who had inevitably become attached to it.

Apart from a passion for AFL and Test cricket, he had no way of occupying his time. He read nothing apart from the sports pages of the papers, didn't want to travel and would only spend a short time gardening under intense pressure from my mother. Yet he constructed an elaborate series of rules to be observed around the house—no one was allowed to wear shoes indoors, no radios were to be played, there was to be no talking at meals, my sister and I were not allowed out of bed on Sunday until he was awake.

Holidays were a nightmare. I still flinch when I drive past the railway hotel in Katoomba. My father used to take the family there for a weekend and then spend the entire time sleeping. No bushwalks, no local restaurants, no cinemas, nothing. My sister and I were told to stay in our room, where we played endless games of Monopoly, interrupted only by occasional trips to the window to watch the passing steam trains.

By 1970 he was so depressed that the doctors recommended a leucotomy. I returned from England to discuss this with them and it was performed in 1971. Overall, it was successful, changing him from a morose introvert into a chatty, carefree extrovert. I had suddenly acquired a new parent with a strikingly different personality.

2007

Out of Toongabbie

We went to Toongabbie—my parents, my sister and myself—in 1948. The name sounds exotic, some old Aboriginal meeting place on the banks of an outback river, but in fact it's only thirty kilometres west of Sydney. The area is flat and hot and in those days it was a new suburb, with roads hurriedly splayed through the ti-tree scrub and thousands of flimsy and near-identical houses. Coming from Springwood, in the Blue Mountains, I hated it. We moved into an ugly fibro Housing Commission house on a dusty road. It was a long walk from the station. We often walked that walk, the four of us stretched out as if on safari. Because my father couldn't be on time for anything, we usually missed the train and then had to wait hours for another or—more commonly—simply trudged back home again.

I spent three years at the local primary school, The Meadows, now vast and modern but consisting in the late 1940s of a two-room brick building which held all six classes. A couple of years ago a memorial booklet of the school arrived at my apartment in London. Somehow, someone had tracked me down. I looked through it and found a photograph labelled 'Students in 1950'. A group of boys are staring towards the camera, most of them with impish grins. No one was identified and I couldn't recall any of the faces—apart from one. In the middle of the photograph was myself at ten. Smiling shyly, hair combed flat (later it went curly, then it fell out), buck teeth (later laboriously straightened) and a long neck (I still have that).

I spend very little time examining the past, probably because recalling my numerous mistakes and mistreatment of so many people would be too depressing, but on a flight to Los Angeles I spent hours studying the rather well-produced little book about that strange little primary school. I tried to recall some of my classmates. I was proud that a few came back to me over the fifty-year gap: Tom Lang, rough and likable, whose feet were deformed in some strange way. They faced one another, which didn't stop

Tom being a dynamic rugby player and even a runner. Tom Dengate, a big boy with rust-coloured eyes who wore tight shorts summer and winter, was always barefoot, and had a huge dog that followed him everywhere. Malcolm Dennett, thin and intense—he always seemed to know everything and was rumoured to have the highest schoolboy IQ in the state. And Doug Timmins, good-looking, cheerful and fearless—willing to tangle with any of the many bullies who roamed the area.

I vividly remember my teacher, as one always does. The irascible Mr Muscio caned me so hard and so often, but was also so patient and so encouraging. He kept assuring me that, despite my low IQ, I had a bright future. He told us one day that we would see the year 2000, that he wouldn't make it and that the world would be greatly changed. It seemed so far in the future on that hot summer day, in an era when we rushed outside to look at an aeroplane flying over, that I couldn't imagine it ever arriving—yet the time passed in an instant.

A number of migrant kids began arriving in 1950 and we were instructed to treat them just like anyone else. This seemed rather harsh but I suppose the war in Europe and subsequent transit camps had more or less prepared them for the rigours of Toongabbie. I recall an odd silent boy named Barrett, from Malta, whose quietness gave him such an air of menace that even the most violent of the school bullies, the vicious and sinister Mavern (whose *spécialité de la maison* was peeing over defeated rivals—forced to lie on the ground—after a cricket match), left him alone. Barrett showed no interest whatever in schoolwork and eventually the teachers seemed to abandon all efforts with him.

Much more vivacious was a tall girl from Estonia with strong Slavic features, Dzintra Ulm, who aroused in me, for the first time, strange and wild emotions. Her English was assured yet wonderfully fractured and I remember she wanted to be a hairdresser, even at the age of ten.

I hope that Dzintra achieved her ambition. I hope they have all done well, except Mavern. It seems strange to me how completely they have all disappeared from my life. I encountered none of them in high school or university and sometimes wonder, as I move around the world, if one of them could be nearby. A few, no doubt, would have dropped off the perch, but most must be still around—grandparents, the majority, with a variety of stories of success, failure, lost loves and tragic deaths—but still around. I'm always half-expecting a tap on the shoulder and then a vaguely familiar face telling me that we went to primary school together—in Toongabbie.

From time to time, every five years or so, I have lunch in Sydney with the one person from Toongabbie, Brian Larking, with whom I've maintained contact, however intermittent. A month or so ago we met at a fashionable restaurant in Darling Harbour. Two big, ageing, balding, somewhat overweight blokes, both with adult children, both reasonably successful in our various fields. We talked at length about The Meadows primary school, of the Toongabbie of 1950, but seemed to remember entirely different people. I had no recollection of those he described to me, and vice versa. Until I mentioned Margaret Duncan. Petite, blonde Margaret Duncan, her pale blue eyes, her hair so fair as to be almost white, her manner so gentle she spoke always in a whisper.

My friend blushed. 'Margaret Duncan,' he said. 'You know, I was in love with Margaret Duncan.'

I didn't say anything. I didn't tell him, but I was in love with her, too.

2009

The End of the Roxy

I was interested to read an account recently of a proposal to demolish most of the old Roxy Theatre in Parramatta in order to build 'a twenty-storey residential and apartment tower'.

This will be a sad end for a bizarre but attractive architectural oddity which seems destined, in the age of small multiplexes and the ubiquity of films on streaming networks, to join those masterpieces of kitsch that once thrilled me: the St James, Prince Edward and Regent theatres in Sydney. At least the flamboyantly baroque State and Capitol have been kept and restored.

Growing up around Parramatta, my weekend highlight was inevitably a visit to one of that city's movie theatres, despite the objections of my parents, who saw film-going as sinful without ever being able to explain this point of view with rationality. My mother told me, haughtily, that 'servants went to the films.' We never had any servants and lived in a modest house, so I don't know how she acquired this information.

Every Monday, on my way to school, I walked under the bridge which carried the railway line over Church Street, where I could view the enormous posters which advertised the new film that week for the Roxy and the Astra. Even at the age of twelve I would seek out the name of the director to see if it was someone who met with my critical approval.

The Roxy screened the more costly commercial films. I still remember how excited I was to climb the steps of that vaguely Mexican/Moorish palace to see *Samson and Delilah*. It was essential to be early for almost any performance as cinemas in the 1950s, unlike today, always seemed to be packed to capacity. I also recall being told by some adult filmgoer that the steps, before the Second World War, were made of glass and that underneath were trees and flowers, which could be viewed by arriving patrons as they ascended to the theatre. The glass steps were then demolished because of the possibility of the Japanese dropping bombs on them. I accepted this story for many years but later decided it couldn't possibly be correct. Glass steps? Unlikely.

The Astra was a smaller theatre that screened more specialised films and would be classified today almost as an 'art house'. It wasn't built on the grand scale of the Roxy, but was quietly tasteful, with a carpeted upstairs lounge area complete with sofas. The clientele was definitely more refined. Many of the films shown were English; and in those days English films lacked the American brashness that now characterises most of them. My most vivid memory of my Astra film-going was the screening, which must have been in 1953 or 1954, of John Ford's *The Sun Shines Bright.* Ford's telling of this simple story, set in one of the Southern states of America just after the Civil War, was told with such warmth and charm that I decided on the spot that I wanted to be a film director when I grew up, so that I could tell stories that would move and entertain people just as they had moved and entertained me.

I imagined the Astra was demolished many years ago. In fact, a quick check on Google reveals it survived until 1986.

Almost opposite the Roxy was another theatre, the Civic, which was the largest of the three Parramatta theatres. Unlike the other two, though, it was just a big box and quite unadorned. On Saturday afternoons it had a noisy audience of children, as it ran three serials. Apart from a couple of visits I was no fan of these—being contemptuous of their woeful plots and tawdry production values.

Apart from this, the Civic screened mostly B films and revivals, much to my delight. I remember having to put enormous pressure on my parents to let me visit the Civic to see revival screenings of 1930s or 1940s films, usually on the double bill which was standard perhaps up until the early 1960s. If the old films had Ronald Colman, Henry Fonda or Errol Flynn in the lead my father usually gave in and mumbled a grudging okay to my request. It was at the Civic that I learnt to appreciate the skills of B-film directors such as Phil Karlson, Don Siegel, Budd Boetticher and Burt Kennedy, all of whom have now been acclaimed by critics internationally, but were dismissed as tenth-rate when I saw their films as a schoolboy.

I believe that the Civic was turned into an office block some years ago. The Astra has gone, so it will be a shame if the Roxy, which was altered when turned into a multiplex in 1976, also disappears. The admirable 'developers' are promising to keep a fragment of the exotic Mexican façade to remind old duffers like me of the grand days of 'the pictures'—and the visits to a quasi-palace to see them.

2015

The Lure of the EH

It must have been sometime in 1975, on the Pacific Highway at St Leonards. I nearly ran off the road when I spotted a 1963 EH Holden in a car yard. I'm not sure why I had always found this model appealing; perhaps it was because it vaguely resembled a miniaturised version of the American cars of the 1950s I admired.

Around nine hundred dollars changed hands. It seemed a lot to me at the time, but I had just signed a contract to direct a film of David Williamson's play *Don's Party* and was thrilled to be receiving a ten-thousand-dollar fee—though, in retrospect, it was not all that spectacular for a year's work, even in the 1970s. I was, however, intent on establishing a little critical credibility after the hammering I'd taken with two Barry McKenzie films.

I know that now the EJ and EH Holdens are much sought-after (a quick browse on Google reveals they sell for anything from twenty thousand to thirty-five thousand dollars), but at that time this was not the case. I remember a rather furtive salesman looking at me with curiosity as I walked purposefully around my new purchase, hoping, undoubtedly in vain, to give the impression of someone who was not simply an impulse buyer.

The exterior two-tone gunmetal grey was profoundly unexciting, but the 1950s American Chrysler-style dashboard and, especially, the purple-and-silver vinyl seats were a joyous counterpoint. These stretched gaudily across the front and rear—none of this individual-aeroplane-seat nonsense with headrests that are all the rage these days, a development originated, no doubt, by some misogynist, a man deeply unappealing to women who resented the thought of attractive girlfriends, or possibly even wives, snuggling up right next to the driver with their right hand resting, arousingly, on his left thigh as he skilfully manoeuvred the EH through city traffic.

The next five or six years were a delight. The EH was driven all over New South Wales and Victoria with never a hint of a mechanical problem. In fact, the engine was incredibly simple in comparison with cars built after the year 2000, where there are so many bits and pieces that mechanics need PhDs to be able to carry out minor adjustments. Even then they'd be stuck without access to computer diagnostics.

A further delight was the exceptional vision from the interior. Huge front and rear windows provided perfect views of all the other vehicles on the road. Modern cars are a definite step backwards in this area. Now, tiny windows give the driver the miniaturised panorama of a Second World War tank commander, entombed under a cupola with a peephole. The side mirrors on modern cars are a further trap (there were none on the EH), as they are aligned with a lethal blind spot, which leads inevitably to minor collisions and scrapes, providing plenty of opportunity to witness otherwise normal people insane with road rage.

Perhaps the only modern addition meriting my endorsement is the now ubiquitous air-conditioning. I remember a number of EH outback trips in over one hundred degrees Fahrenheit (otherwise known as thirty-three degrees Celsius—another unwelcome change) with the only faint relief being the air (hot) blowing in from a small side window that could be angled onto the driver. I invariably ignored the screams of my three children sitting on the back seat as their sweating legs became stuck to the vinyl.

...

In 1979 I directed the film *Breaker Morant* to considerable critical acclaim. After two decades in the film industry, I was an overnight success. Despite the critical enthusiasm, *Breaker Morant* was ignored by vast audiences worldwide. I found out recently its box-office takings now total $4 million, a figure it has taken thirty-four years to reach. My film *Double Jeopardy*, released in 1999, which never had a single favourable review, took $26 million in its opening week.

In Los Angeles, *Breaker Morant* screened for only two days in a decrepit theatre (now closed) on Wilshire Boulevard, so I was surprised to be sent a number of scripts by Hollywood executives. It turned out the film was showing as an in-flight movie on the LA–NYC run, so my directorial skills were on display to a captive audience.

From the numerous scripts sent to me (no email in those days) I selected a beautifully written drama by the playwright Horton Foote, *Tender Mercies.* I found out only a couple of years ago that this simple story, set in Texas, of a country-and-western singer and his girlfriend, had been turned down by a gaggle of American directors—luckily for me. The film had five Academy Award nominations in 1983, including one for me as Best Director. It won two awards: Best Actor (Robert Duvall) and Best Screenplay.

I am now moving rather lugubriously to the point of this recap of my film career. The move to the United States to make a film clearly meant I would be leaving the adored

EH for some time—for some years, as it turned out. I knew it would rot away if left in a garage untended so I managed, after an extensive search without the aid of Google, to find a place on the outskirts of Sydney where the car could be left in the company of other vehicles. The somewhat feral owners of this property assured me the car would be started up from time to time, and cobwebs and various nesting marsupials would be removed.

Tender Mercies was filmed in 1982, another American film followed, and I didn't return to Australia until sometime in 1986. The day after landing I managed to find my way out to the bush car-resting home. The EH looked a bit grimy, but there was no rust and the engine started instantly. I drove back to the city, lovingly washed the car and RE-POed the glorious two-tone grey duco. (RE-PO was the polish of that time; Google tells me it still exists.) I was aware that the cost of a couple of years' garaging was considerably more than the value of the car, but...I had it back.

Once again, the EH reliably carted my family and me all over New South Wales. We often visited my uncle's farm near Coolah, where the EH proved to be the master, having such high clearance, of the miles of pot-holed roads, bush tracks, innumerable gullies, and even paddocks strewn with logs and rabbit warrens.

A couple of years later I was off to America again, this time to direct *Driving Miss Daisy* (1989), another small-scale drama with, like *Tender Mercies*, a cast of only three significant roles. Again, it was predicted that this low-budget film would sink without trace. Instead, it rose without trace: being modestly financed by a Canadian producer and having no 'star' names in the cast. Jessica Tandy was a stage actress, and Morgan Freeman had previously only had a supporting role in one film. It surprised everyone, myself included, with nine Academy Award nominations in 1990. It won four, including Best Picture.

Despite an improvement in my financial situation, I was not prepared to contemplate returning the EH to the farmyard for abandoned cars. I had, after all, been directing essentially art-house films and not the blockbusters that would have ensured the yacht, the house in Elizabeth Bay and the holiday villa in Saint-Tropez.

With a lot of hesitation, I acceded to my father's entreaties to leave the car with him while I was overseas. At least there was a garage at my parents' house at Kurrajong Heights, about eighty kilometres from Sydney, so I wouldn't be paying out thousands of dollars a year while in America. The drawback was that, like all terrible drivers, my father was quite convinced that he was the sole person on the road who drove well. Ever since a horrific trip to a boat race at the age of ten—during which the police had booked him three times for speeding—I had refused to travel in a car when he was driving and, some years later, forbade my three children to let him drive them anywhere, no matter how he pleaded.

It was true he was now car-less in Kurrajong. (My mother, who had died about a year previously, had put her foot down about him being behind the wheel of anything with an engine some time prior to this sad event.) In fact, he even had trouble walking and imperiously refused the use of a cane to help his balance, preferring to fall over regularly.

He pointed out, in his defence, that he'd never had a serious car accident and dismissed the numerous 'non-serious' ones as the fault of other idiots behind the wheel. He even classed as 'non-serious' the time he drove well over the speed limit the wrong direction down a one-way street and hit another vehicle head-on. Amazingly, no one was hurt in either car, which he saw as justifying his assertion of a 'minor accident'.

His licence had been revoked a number of times, but he assured me he had it back once again. I doubted, and still doubt, that this was true, but weakly gave in to his ultimate argument that he would be driving nowhere but three or four miles up the road—a quiet country road—to the bowling club and back again. And there was, I knew, little chance that he would plunge over a cliff while inebriated. If alcohol had been added to his already tenuous driving skills, I would have been forced to park the EH once again with the feral caretakers.

...

After some months in America, I had to return to Sydney for meetings. As our house was rented out, I checked into a hotel at the airport for the duration of my brief visit. The moment I entered my room I dived to the phone to call my father in Kurrajong. I had spoken to him a couple of times from Los Angeles and he had assured me tersely that the EH was running perfectly and being cared for faultlessly. I was unconvinced, as I remembered various cars of his from my childhood. They all quickly resembled mobile rubbish tips, were never washed and had endless mechanical problems through neglect.

This time a voice on the phone told me the number had been disconnected. I began to panic. Had he suddenly died? Was he lying on the living-room floor, unable to move? Or, most likely, had he simply failed to pay the phone bill, just as he had habitually ignored any envelopes with little transparent windows all his life? Plagued by the various possibilities, I immediately set out for Kurrajong Heights in a rented car.

It was dusk when I arrived at the house, but I could see that my mother's formerly well-tended garden was a weed-infested shambles. The EH was parked outside not in the garage and, in the gloom, it seemed to be in one piece. The lights of Sydney glimmered in the distance, but the house itself was in darkness. Now very apprehensive, fearing the worst, I went to the front door. It was stuck, though partially ajar, and the glass was smashed. Unable to move it, I went to the side door leading to the kitchen. It opened easily, and I walked through into the living room. The television was the only light source. My father was sitting on a sofa watching cricket. He greeted me casually and went on watching.

I slept that night in the musty spare room and rushed outside early to look closely at the EH. It was free of the minor dents that usually characterised his cars, but the seats were full of newspapers and a few old sweaters. On its exterior there was still no rust, just plenty of grime. The windows were filthy and the duco was oddly mottled and discoloured. I never succeeded in finding out how this had happened in the six months or so I'd been away, though I realised the car had never been parked in the garage as it was too full of old newspapers to allow space for this.

A couple of days later, despite his protests, I took the EH away. In fact, he protested a lot less than I expected, so I suspect that the local policeman had seen him driving and issued a warning to desist.

A few miles down the road, somewhere near the town of Richmond, I found a car wash and drove through it. I then emptied the seats of the old newspapers and bits of assorted rubbish, mostly wrappers for chocolate bars. Prompted by an odd smell I looked under the driver's seat and found a vast pile of Kentucky Fried Chicken bones. I knew my father was addicted to this delicacy, and I suppose I shouldn't have been surprised that he considered putting the bones under the seat more sensible than throwing them into a bin.

Once the car was clean, inside and out, it seemed to run more smoothly. I had noticed over the years that cars always seemed to do this, though it makes no logical sense.

Back in Sydney, I contacted an out-of-work actor of my acquaintance who I knew had a car respraying business on the side. He did a far better job than I expected, probably because he had realised the car-spraying business was far more profitable than thespianism. I even toyed with dispensing with the gunmetal grey in favour of brighter colours, but the actor/sprayer insisted that would take too long and he had little time as he was expecting a major role to be coming his way.

The EH was now, unlike my father, in showroom condition. There was no rust, the engine ran like new and I could see the admiring glances as I drove around the city. However, a disposal question arose once again when I had to return to America to work on my next film. This time I decided I had to sell the car. My international career had moved from non-existent to sporadic and I suspected, barring a one-hundred-per-cent critical disaster, I could be out of Australia for quite a few years.

I contacted a valuation service run by the NRMA and was stunned to be told the car was worth only around four hundred dollars. I pointed out that this was no old wreck but an impeccable vehicle. It made no difference. It was reiterated to me that four hundred dollars would be the best I could expect.

Over the years I have sold many cars, usually because of overseas travel, and every one of them has been meticulously maintained: my old VW (my first car), my Citroën DS (sold because patriotic Australians bravely threw stones at it during the French bombing tests in the Pacific), my Jaguar, my Subaru and the Mercedes I bought in Adelaide while filming *Breaker Morant*. I realise now I must be one of the few people who is so scrupulous. I read a newspaper article that insisted that *most* cars in used-car yards have some disastrous fault that has necessitated their sale. A used-car salesman told me once in a moment of rare honesty that a good test when buying is to switch on the car radio. If it is tuned to a classical station such as ABC FM, then the car is most likely to be in good condition. A rock station or talk-back programme is a warning sign to look for an alternative vehicle.

Unwilling to give away my beautiful, gleaming, mechanically perfect EH for four hundred dollars, I offered it, as a gift, to a young cousin who had recently moved to Sydney from Brisbane. On the day I went back to the United States he drove me to the airport in it. I'm always being told I'm not the sentimental type, but there were tears in my eyes as I lifted my case from the boot and walked into the terminal. I never saw the EH again.

My cousin reported that he drove the car for some

years, then disposed of it. I don't know the details and urged him not to tell me. I still tremble with excitement when the occasional EH (I always look for the numberplate EH599) passes my field of vision, although reason tells me my car, now over fifty years old, is probably rusting away unhappily or has been compacted into a metal oblong.

My father went to an old folk's home near Geelong—not far from my sister, who had moved to Melbourne. He seemed happy there. He died quietly about a year later, shortly after watching an AFL game on television.

I'm now driving a 2002 Lexus, a first-rate car, but without the magic of my EH. Now in my seventies, I am still directing films and operas, though I seem to spend a lot of time going to the funerals of my contemporaries.

At Bills Garage in Balmain, where the Lexus is serviced, I have noticed, a few times, a flawless EH: the same model as mine but more vibrantly coloured. Enquiries revealed that it's owned by a lady who has no intention of selling. The garage owner is under instruction to call me the moment that she decides to dispose of this gem.

2013

In Guatemala

Los Angeles, 1982. I was in town to direct a film and suddenly found myself, because of a sudden coup in the studio hierarchy, with a spare week. My film was put on hold while the new heads decided (a) whether to proceed with it at all and (b) if the decision was made to proceed, would there be, perhaps, a change of director?

I decided that this was an ideal time to make a visit to Guatemala. I had long wanted to see the Mayan ruins at Tikal. This was before the days when travel bookings were laboriously made on the internet, so I visited my local travel agent and bought three tickets for the following day—for myself, my son (age thirteen) and my daughter (age fifteen).

We turned up in plenty of time in an obscure section of Los Angeles airport. All went smoothly until I was asked for our visas. I had been told, I explained, that visas weren't necessary for Guatemala. Quite wrong. Could I get the visas here at the airport? Impossible. They could only be obtained from the Guatemalan Embassy in downtown Los Angeles.

Back to our house in Los Feliz. The next morning I was given the address of the embassy and drove downtown early so that I could be there when it opened at, I assumed, 9.00 a.m.

The address turned out to be in a particularly rundown part of the city. Every second store sold liquor, the streets were strewn with rubbish and the passers-by were sadly down at heel. It took me some time to locate the correct number of the embassy building and, when I did, it proved to be a huge hole in the ground. I stared at it in an understandable state of bewilderment, as this was unquestionably the address given to me by someone on the embassy staff.

After a few minutes a Latino man passing by asked if I wanted the Guatemalan Embassy. Many people, he said, came to the address of this huge hole. He couldn't understand why this was, when the embassy had moved two years previously. Luckily, he knew the new address and wrote it down for me.

The new embassy was a few streets away. It was just one room in a broken-down office building. Although the room was full of what looked like very disgruntled Guatemalans, slouching in uncomfortable chairs, the visas were stamped into the three passports within a few minutes.

The next day we flew to Guatemala City, rented a car and drove to the old capital of Antigua, which proved to be one of world's most beautiful cities, having the stunning architecture, gardens, churches, houses and squares characteristic of so many Spanish colonial towns. I kept hidden from my son and daughter a printed warning I had picked up from the Australian Consulate in Los Angeles, urging me to 'exercise a high degree of caution. Guatemala has a high crime rate. Criminals have targeted tourists arriving at the international airport and travelling to hotels in Antigua.'

After a couple of glorious days of sightseeing and meetings with no one but friendly locals, we drove back to Guatemala City and caught a small plane to an airport near Tikal. Both the plane and airport reminded me of Howard Hawks' 1939 masterpiece *Only Angels Have Wings*, with its unflattering but vivid recreation of a banana republic. I realised that the Hollywood version of Central America wasn't too wide of the mark.

The one-room arrival lounge quickly emptied of the few passengers, leaving us in the company of a louche black girl. Intending to ring to check on our hire car, I asked, 'Do you have a phone?' (This was the pre-mobile era, of course.)

Lazily, she reached under the bench she was slumped across and produced a vintage black telephone, covered in dust. There was no dial tone. 'This phone doesn't seem to work,' I said. 'No,' she replied, 'but you said, "Do you have a phone?"'

The hire car arrived a few minutes later. With my son navigating, we headed down an appropriately pot-holed road towards Tikal. My daughter read from the guidebook a section which strongly advised against staying in the huts at the historic site itself, as they weren't clean, the food was terrible, the organisation a shambles. I'd decided to risk it regardless, as the nearest hotel was so distant.

As is so often the case, the guidebook was in error. The accommodation, though not luxurious, was clean and comfortable, the food plain but tasty and the English-speaking lady who seemed to be in charge of everything associated with Tikal was delighted to have three such enthusiastic guests. (My faith in guidebooks plummeted further when my wife and I decided to take a tour in the south of France. Toulouse, our book assured us, was a dump with nothing worth seeing. Further, the surrounding area was a bore. This was a long way from the truth.)

After we'd spent a few days clambering over the spectacular ruins—me pretending to my children that I was not terrified to follow them up steep narrow staircases and then to walk along narrow crumbling brickwork with a sheer drop on both sides—the lady in charge of everything asked if we'd like to visit another Mayan city a few miles away. There is no other Mayan city nearby, I smugly assured her, having read all the material on the Maya I could find. I backed this up by producing a local map, which showed no other Mayan city anywhere near Tikal.

She put the three of us in her Land Rover and we headed off along a jungle track. An hour or so later we emerged into a large clearing with huge and totally unrestored ruins. A number of men were idly sitting around on the remnants of temples. 'What do they do for a living?' I asked. There were no towns around and no farms. 'They rob tombs,' was the answer.

Friends greeted us back in Los Angeles a few days later with cries of relief. 'We're so glad you're safe,' we were told. 'The coup in Guatemala has been all over the papers and television. The country is in uproar. Thousands are dead.' Evidently someone with the suitably sinister name of General Efraín Ríos Montt had taken over the country while we were there, an event that managed to bypass me.

I seem to be able to march obliviously through turmoil—perhaps I inherited a strange gene from my father, who had been baffled by the outbreak of the Second World War. I was on holiday in Paris during the 1968 riots and was unaware of anything amiss. I was in Enugu, Nigeria, during a military coup in 1964 and noticed nothing out of the ordinary.

Whatever the reason, our introduction to Guatemala was blissfully benevolent and peaceful. Everyone we met had been friendly—except the lady with the phone, and she was more bored and indifferent than hostile.

2011

Pass the Passport

February 2003. I was in Los Angeles editing a film. I called my son, Benjamin, in Normandy and suggested he visit for a few weeks. He told me that he'd lost his Australian passport, so I pointed out he could use his British passport (Benjamin was born in England, in 1967, while I was working there) and I would arrange for a new Australian one. This would be easy, I assured him, as people must lose their passports all the time.

A couple of days later I called the Australian consular office in Los Angeles and was told it was closing down in an economy drive. They gave me the number of the office in Washington, DC. I phoned the Washington office, explained what had happened and was told the appropriate forms would be sent to me.

A few days later the forms arrived. I filled them in, had Benjamin sign them (Benjamin has Down's syndrome and needs help with many tasks, though the intricacy of the forms would have taxed Alan Turing) and sent them off to Washington.

A few weeks later the forms were returned along with a note saying, briefly, that the passport had to be renewed in Canberra. I had, the note added, filled in the wrong forms in any case. There was no acknowledgment that these were in fact the forms sent in response to my request.

Then everything collapsed on the film I was editing. HBO, the production company, didn't like my version of it and I was subtly divested of control. The role of bystander didn't appeal and I decided to return to Australia for a few months, leaving the film in the skilled hands of the HBO executives.

Back in Sydney, I sent the passport forms off to Canberra, as instructed. Once again they came back. This time there was a follow-up phone call to tell me that the passport had to be renewed in England or France, as it was lost when Benjamin was in Europe. This seemed odd to me, but I was assured that Benjamin simply had to turn up at Australia House in the Strand and he'd be given a new passport. All his details would be on the computer.

A few weeks later I had to go to London for meetings about a couple of films I was fairly sure would never find finance—one of them an exciting script about the Everest climber George Mallory, written by Jeffrey Archer; the other a tough drama about the Angolan war, written by a South African named Paul Herzberg—but at least I'd be able to sort out the passport.

With an unwilling and somewhat baffled Benjamin in tow, I turned up at Australia House at 9.30 one morning. The passport and visa office was in a side entrance of the building. I was told to take a numbered ticket and sit on a pew to wait for the interview. A number of backless wooden benches were set out, facing the same direction. These were already packed with people when we arrived, all sitting silently, staring. Benjamin and I joined them.

I read the morning newspaper and then looked around. There appeared to have been no movement at all. The same glum crowd were in the same positions. I felt we were all in Lisbon, 1941, trying to get exit visas from wartime Europe. The person or persons doing the interviews could not actually be seen, as they were in a booth at right angles to the seated applicants. I now watched the procedure with more interest, not to say a sense of foreboding.

It didn't take long to work out that only one person was conducting the interviews. Further, each applicant whose number was called spent an average of twenty-five minutes with the interviewer. I counted the number of people in the room and worked out, even with my appalling maths, that our interview would take place around midnight.

I went back to the entrance of the room and spoke to an official dressed in the uniform of a highly decorated member of a Ruritanian army. He was jovial and agreed with my calculations, the only drawback being that the office closed at 5 p.m. In other words, they were handing out tickets to people they already knew had no hope of being seen that day. Did the numbers carry over to the next day? No. The next day was a fresh start.

I waited a couple of hours more, just to see if the pace of the interviews would pick up. It didn't. So I nudged Benjamin and indicated we were leaving. At the entrance I bumped into a young Australian backpacker and asked if he knew any shortcuts to the interviewer. Oh yes, he said, you have to be here about 7 a.m. Without one of the first half-dozen tickets you're sunk, mate.

The next morning I dragged an extremely unwilling and now hostile Benjamin out of bed and we walked down to the Strand from my Bloomsbury flat. It was about 7.15 when we arrived but there were already four people in the line. It was cold, but at least not raining. I looked around for a coffee shop, but the only one I could see, some distance away, was enterprisingly closed. In order to keep Benjamin entertained we played Botticelli—a word game which relies on extensive general knowledge to be fun. Benjamin's general knowledge is limited but his knowledge of films, their actors and directors, is formidable, and we occupied our time until 9.30 with attempts to find, for example, the famous F who directed *The Narrow Margin* in the early 1950s (Fleischer, Richard). When I challenged Benjamin to name the brilliantly gifted film director whose initials were BB he quickly said, 'Bernardo Bertolucci.'

At precisely 9.30 the Ruritanian war hero opened the door and there was a mad scramble for the little tickets. By now the queue had grown to at least fifty people. I grabbed the fourth ticket and once again we took our places on the spartan benches.

A mere couple of hours later Benjamin and I rounded the corner to the interviewer's booth. The interviewer turned out to be an attractive and pleasant young woman from Brisbane. She put Benjamin's name into the computer. All his details were there...yes, he was an Australian, he'd had two passports, went to school in Sydney in the 1970s, and so on. Of course he could have a new passport, but this couldn't be issued in London. It couldn't? No, it could only be issued in Sydney.

Trying hard to give the appearance of a calm and totally rational person I outlined the story so far. The young lady listened attentively, then went into a back room. She was gone for some time, perhaps twenty minutes. When she came back, she told us that they could give Benjamin a passport valid for one year. Back in Sydney, all that had to be done was to present it at a post office and it would be changed for a standard passport. This all seemed strange, but no stranger, I supposed, than previous episodes of the passport saga. The photographs of Benjamin, she told us, were unacceptable, and it was necessary to go to a photographer for new ones. She gave me an address. The photographer took the photos, which looked identical to me, and I returned these to the consulate. The next day we collected the one-year passport.

We were back in Sydney in April 2004. I took Benjamin, with his one-year passport, into a large post office. The passport was examined. It was passed from hand to hand, then given back to us with the information that it was necessary to have 'evidence of Australian citizenship'. This was a certificate that had to be produced before any passport could be issued. Why had no one mentioned this before? Odd, as it's essential. How long would it take to get one? Perhaps four weeks from the time it was requested. But, I pointed out (still calm and rational), Benjamin would by then have returned to his mother's house in France. This wouldn't matter, I was assured, all I would need was the citizenship certificate and a photocopy of the one-year passport—then the full passport would be issued.

A few weeks later the colourful and rather attractive 'Evidence of Australian Citizenship' certificate arrived, emblazoned with the coat of arms of the Commonwealth, a big red seal and the statement that Benjamin Gordon Nash Beresford 'is an Australian citizen and that citizenship was acquired on 22nd July 1986'.

Convinced, foolishly, that this epic saga was approaching an end, I returned to the post office. Everything was carefully examined and I was asked why Benjamin's credit cards or his Medicare number were not listed. I explained that I'd written a letter to accompany the application form, pointing out that he had Down's syndrome and was unable to deal with credit cards. He had no Medicare card, as his medical bills were taken care of as a dependant through the Directors Guild of America.

A phone call was made to someone in the main office at Railway Square. A lady curtly told me there was a need to prove Benjamin's existence. I explained that I had brought him into the post office originally, that we had the citizenship certificate and a photograph signed by a JP who had known him for fourteen years. What about more evidence of his residency in Australia? What sort of evidence? Would it be sufficient if I supplied information from his primary school in Epping and his high school, St Andrews? No, this wouldn't be acceptable.

The long conversation was getting nowhere. The entire post office staff and half a dozen customers were listening with interest. With a massive effort of will, I prevented myself from screaming or weeping and collapsing into a pathetic heap on the floor.

In a neat coup de grâce the lady told me that the passport could only be issued in London. We had tried in London, I explained, and were told it had to be issued in Sydney. Well, she said, that's because they didn't actually *see* Benjamin in London. But they did see him! Well, you must've filled in the wrong forms, she insisted—rather gleefully, I thought. I filled in the forms I was told were the correct ones for someone who had lost his passport…

An appointment was arranged for me to talk to someone at the head office in Railway Square. The ticket system operated here, too, but more than one person was handling all the enquiries. In less than half an hour I was explaining the whole mess all over again to a friendly Indian-born man, who listened attentively. He, too, was adamant that the passport could only be issued in London, but this was a simple matter. They—the Sydney office—would forward all the documentation, the photographs, the certificates, the note from the JP, the letters and the rest, and all I would have to do is turn up with Benjamin and collect the passport.

Early the next year I was in London again, but Benjamin had collapsed at Heathrow after the flight back from Sydney and was in hospital with a blood clot in his leg. I think he was relieved not to be dragged immediately back to Australia House.

A few months later he'd recovered but by then I was in Bulgaria (was my career on the skids?) preparing an elaborate thriller to star Morgan Freeman and John Cusack. Anticipating that I'd be in London at the end of the shoot, I thought it worthwhile to email Australia House just to check that all the forms had arrived. Not much chance they wouldn't have, I naively thought, as about eight months had gone by. However, a courteous reply from Australia House told me that 'to date no papers have been passed to us.' This was followed by information telling me how to get a new passport for Benjamin.

Clearly, the entire process has to begin all over again. Benjamin and I would have to return to that drab little room off the side entrance to Australia House, where the Orwellian battle for the passport will continue. Not so much continue as begin, as the two and a half years already spent counts for nothing.

Having worked all over the world, I've always thought of Australia as an efficient country where everything happens with a minimum of bureaucracy and fuss. Yet this passport saga is something worthy of the administrative system of an African republic or the old communist countries of Eastern Europe.

...

After I wrote the above, I applied once again for Benjamin's passport through the honorary Australian consul in Sofia. All the information was supplied once again, exactly the same as before; the material was sent off to the embassy in Athens. A week or two later a call came to say that the application appeared to be in order, and a few days after that, in mid-August, the passport was issued.

2005

The Age of Memoirs

I have now reached the age which seems to prompt various of my university contemporaries to write a memoir. I find it hard to believe that most of these would have huge appeal outside the group (Sydney University, 1959–62) being recalled, though Clive James's autobiography—into its fifth volume—is witty or, more accurately, hilarious, and Bob Hughes's *Things I Didn't Know* is ruthlessly honest, even lacerating in the account of his disastrous first marriage. Germaine Greer, needless to say, is a worldwide celebrity with a huge swag of books, public lectures and television appearances. Controversial (she seems to approve of clitoridectomies on the grounds that they are traditional in certain cultures) and often brashly irritating, she taught my sister at high school for some months. My sister gave her top marks as a teacher, saying that she was stimulating, thoughtful, interested in her pupils and brilliant at conveying her passion for literature.

People often comment to me that the early 1960s at Sydney University was an era of remarkable personalities and achievement. This acclaimed (usually self-acclaimed) group was concerned almost exclusively with the arts. I am certain that students who contributed more to society in the fields of medicine, science, the law and even politics have been overlooked.

Albie Thoms' memoir, *My Generation* (2012), strongly recalls the man himself. He and I were never great friends but always good ones. He had a relaxed, even charming manner, showed no envy and invariably displayed a remarkably equitable temperament. I assumed that this pleasant manner was the reason numerous young women found him attractive, while they ignored the more tormented figures such as myself. Though he became associated with the avant-garde (he championed the obscure plays of the diminutive Spaniard Arrabal and the tedious ones of Samuel Beckett), I was always surprised that, almost alone among the student body, Albie invariably wore a grey suit and tie.

Albie knew virtually everyone in the arts field during

that era and tells a number of anecdotes with enthusiasm and, I can certainly say in relation to those concerning myself, considerable accuracy—although he omits our most dramatic encounter. We had been in Melbourne in connection with some university play. We left quite late at night to return to Sydney, which was ill-advised. Albie was driving and I was asleep in the adjacent front seat. I vividly remember waking as the window to my left hit the ground. I can still hear the sound of smashing glass and crunching metal. The car must have rolled over a few times before ending up in the bush at the side of the road.

The next thing I recall was walking, dazed, among the trees. At some point I had been thrown clear of the car, or else I crawled from the wreck—I've no idea which. Some passing motorists, who I kept insisting were American tourists (perhaps they were, as I recall asking them if we were in America), took me to their car and drove to a small hospital in a nearby town appropriately named Kilmore. I have a hazy memory of a doctor arriving, annoyed at being dragged out of bed in the middle of the night. He put a bandage on my head and disappeared.

The next day we somehow (I don't recall how; Albie's car was a total wreck; he was unharmed) returned to Melbourne and then flew to Sydney. My sister met me at the airport and drove me straight to the family doctor. He looked at my head wound, his invariably calm manner deserting him briefly as he commented, 'I can see your brain.' I'm not sure exactly what he did after that, as I was still disorientated. He told me some months later that he thought I could get some lethal infection, the implication being that the Kilmore doctor was somewhat casual.

Rampaging through the pages of Albie's lengthy work are Germaine Greer as a revue star and lead in a Brecht play, John Bell establishing himself as an actor of genius (one of Albie's few barbed asides brands him as an 'Olivier imitator') and Bob Hughes as a successful painter (a career he wisely abandoned in favour of art criticism), plus a support cast that includes Martin Sharp, Richard Neville, Garry Shead, Leo Schofield, the beautiful Anne O'Neill and Richard Walsh.

The aspect of the recollections which most surprised me, though I suppose it shouldn't have, is the political commentary. Albie was a member of the Sydney Push, an anti-establishment group (many of them not students) that can boast of few attainments other than alcohol consumption and gambling. He expresses surprise that the police would spend a lot of time interrogating a couple of people who were key suspects in the infamous Bogle–Chandler murder case, even though one of them was the husband of the dead woman as well as being a poisons expert (Mr Bogle and Mrs Chandler were poisoned) and the other his current girlfriend. Rather more alarming is the statement that the Push was delighted at the assassination of President Kennedy, whom they 'despised as a warmonger'. Toasts were drunk to the achievement of Lee Harvey Oswald.

Albie died in late 2012, just before his memoir was published, and it was available for the first time at a memorial gathering. There were at least four hundred people present in the town hall at Paddington and many of them, one after another, told touching stories of their love for Albie. A number of old (literally) girlfriends were present, one of whom declared, loudly, 'I was the first one he fucked!'

At the risk of seeming mean-spirited and uncharitable, it strikes me as a little odd that Albie's memorial service would be the venue for considerable acclaim. This is probably a tribute to Albie's agreeable personality. Apart from some plays he directed as a student (I remember him telling me he couldn't really make head or tail of the avant-garde writing of the 1960s but found it appealing nevertheless) there were a few rather amateurish short films; a rather frantic 1980 feature, *Palm Beach*; and a 1984 television film, *Johnny O'Keefe: The Wild One*, co-directed with John Moyle. There seems to be nothing between 1984 and Albie's death.

2013

Inadvertent Meetings—and Premonitions

Inadvertent meetings or strange coincidences don't seem to happen to me anymore, but were quite common until around twenty years ago. I've often puzzled why they petered out.

The first one I remember was in 1963. I had graduated from Sydney University with an unspectacular degree and gone to England. I arranged to meet a university friend, Jim Hirschfeld (who had a spectacular maths degree), soon after arriving, as we had planned a tour around France and

Spain before he began a tutoring post at the University of Edinburgh.

We went to Paris for a week or so, then made our way down to Spain by a combination of buses, trains and hitch-hiking, invariably staying in the cheapest hotels or boarding houses we could find.

Somewhere in the south of Spain we were dropped off by a truck in the middle of an area that looked like the Nullarbor Plain. The driver explained, as far as we could understand, that he was turning onto a side road and could take us no further. He demanded some money from us, rather to our surprise. We paid a modest amount as he and his partner—an uncouth-looking character who could have been from one of Buñuel's Mexican films—were a sinister pair.

The truck lumbered off down a dusty side road and Jim and I proceeded to walk along the dead-straight main road. The countryside was flat and desolate; it was a hot day; there was little vegetation, no houses and no traffic. We trudged along for some miles. In the distance, far in the distance, I could see a cyclist slowly coming towards us.

It must have been twenty minutes before the cyclist reached us. I paid little attention to him, so was startled when he called out, 'Bruce! Jim!' We were stunned to realise this was Ken Horler, a small, intense, dynamic man who had directed both of us in plays at Sydney University. For some reason he had undertaken to cycle around Spain, alone.

After an exchange of touring anecdotes we went our separate ways, Ken in one direction, Jim and I in the other.

...

Ken went back to Sydney, became a successful lawyer and, with the actor John Bell, founded the Nimrod Theatre.

Jim continued his career in maths and was for many years head of the maths department at the University of Sussex. He lives in Brighton and still teaches at Sussex, in between golf tournaments, though past retiring age.

My film career staggered on. Rather to my own surprise I ended up directing and/or writing a number of films.

...

The next unexpected event was around 1967 or 1968.

While a university student I had been fascinated by a girl named Judith. She was olive-skinned and slender, with huge eyes and an alluringly distant manner. I found out many years later that what seemed to be a Garbo-like aloofness was explained simply by the fact that her eyesight was so bad she had difficulty in recognising anyone until they were almost on top of her. No one, as far as I know, was on top of her at this time. She was, I suppose, too vain to wear glasses and contact lenses were a few years away from being in common use.

My pursuit of Judy was fruitless and didn't consist of anything more than an occasional coffee together in the city. Her mother had an annoying habit of showing up, with the intention, I am sure, of escorting Judy out of my presence. Mother, who spoke with an indefinable East European accent, had become suspicious of a lad like myself, who had admitted to living in the unfashionable western suburbs. This attitude was common, I was aware, to most of the mothers of attractive female students. They wanted their daughters to associate with young men from the north shore or eastern suburbs. The fathers, I had also noticed, showed no such interest in geography.

I left Australia in 1963, never expecting to see the beautiful Judith again.

While working for the British Film Institute, I was sent to Venice to show a few reels of a film, *Herostratus*. This was unfinished and was being edited by its director–writer, Don Levy, a charismatic but rather mysterious Australian who claimed to have been a scientist at Cape Canaveral before switching his attention to filmmaking. He had made a couple of highly original documentaries prior to embarking on *Herostratus*, a task which occupied him for many years largely because, in my view, he edited the footage for only a couple of hours each day, rather than the eight to ten hours editors normally spend every day in the cutting room.

I left the reels of the unfinished film with some members of the selection committee for the festival, though

I considered that Don Levy wouldn't have the film finished in time for a screening even if the submitted material was viewed positively. While waiting for a reply—as I had to take the film with me back to London—I spent a few days seeing the sights of Venice.

I was walking over a canal bridge when a tour boat passed underneath. The tour guide was speaking in English. I listened for a few moments as the voice, a woman's voice, sounded familiar. I looked over the railing as the boat passed underneath and saw Judith sitting in the stern, describing the sights to a large group of tourists. I called out to her. She interrupted her description of some palace or other and gave me a time to meet her at the landing place of the tour boats.

I had high expectations of our meeting. Venice, the evening, drinks at a small bar, perhaps an invitation to the modest hotel the British Film Institute had parked me in...

None of this happened. Judy was pleased to see me, clearly, but made sure we were never alone. Perhaps there was a boyfriend with her in Venice? I never found out. After a coffee in St Mark's Square, which seemed to me an echo of our Sydney meetings, though more exotic, we parted.

However, this time there was a coda. Some months later Judy contacted me at the BFI editing rooms, where I was trying to convince Don Levy to put in more hours editing *Herostratus*, which I could see was going to have a running time of at least two and a half hours. Don resisted, clearly under the impression he was already working long hours, though he would turn up in the cutting room around 5 p.m. (and not every day) and leave about 8.

Judy invited me to her flat for dinner. Her husband or boyfriend (I don't know which applies) was out of town. A brief and exciting affair followed, but ceased after a couple of encounters, as both of us were involved in other relationships.

...

I never saw Judy again, though I believe she returned to Australia and worked in some job in the film industry. Her career was always mysterious, at least to me. When we were students I was convinced she had a future as an actress, as I remember her giving a fine performance in a Morris West play at the Independent Theatre, Daughter of Silence. *I've no idea how she shifted from that to being a tour guide in Venice. In London, I think I recall her telling me she was connected with a television series about the houses of the rich and famous. Sadly, she died some years ago, probably only in her fifties.*

Don Levy did eventually finish Herostratus, *which was generally well reviewed in the London press. Technically superb, it was, in my opinion, both pretentious and incomprehensible. Astonishingly, Don was expecting a popular success and was bitterly disappointed when this didn't happen. He was offered a James Bond film to direct but haughtily turned it down as he considered it intellectually beneath him. I urged him to accept it but was wary in pointing out that his great strength as a filmmaker was his startling editing, with an exhilarating feeling for rhythm and juxtaposition of images, not his impenetrable philosophising.*

Don went to America with his German wife and two daughters. He taught at CalArts in Hollywood for some time. He never recovered from the failure of Herostratus. *He committed suicide in 1987.* Herostratus *is available on DVD, though more rewarding is his documentary* Time Is *and a very short film, based on a poem by Christopher Brennan, 'Point of Noon'.*

...

The third inadvertent meeting, or near-meeting, I recall took place in London around 1985. I was driving with my son and daughter along Gloucester Road. There was a lot of traffic, so progress was slow. We were having a politically incorrect conversation about people we knew who were extraordinarily unattractive. Both son and daughter had various suggestions for the gold cup, from among their acquaintances in both Australia and England.

I dismissed their suggestions and proposed a lady I knew in Australia. Neither of them had met her and were dismissive of my claims regarding her lack of physical appeal. Quite suddenly, I had to stop the car because of traffic. Right in front of us, casually crossing the road, was the lady in question. 'I tell you,' I said triumphantly, 'she is the most unattractive person I've known...and...there she is!'

Both kids stared with disbelief at the person indicated. A silence fell. I could tell my candidate was a clear winner.

...

I have always been dismissive of people who claim to have extra-sensory perception and tend to lump them with conspiracy theorists, members of the flat-earth society, and believers in ghosts and flying saucers. I actually had an assistant on one film who subscribed to all of the above.

My mother tended to be a teller of fantastic tales, all dismissed by me as the ravings of someone disappointed by the tough hand life had dealt her: a mentally unstable husband and a life with him in subsidised housing in an upper-lower-class to lower-middle-class suburb.

One of her stories, though, I believed. During the war, she was living with her sister in a flat in the city. Her youngest brother, Bruce, was with the Australian army in New Guinea. One night she woke, having clearly heard him call her name: 'Lona...Lona.' She got out of bed and looked around the flat, then went back to bed. A few minutes later the call came again. This time she went and woke her sister, Betty, and asked if she had heard Bruce calling. Betty had heard nothing.

My mother went back to bed. News came a couple of days later that Bruce had died fighting the Japanese.

...

I have experienced nothing so dramatic, though there are a few incidents that defy any logical explanation.

Around 1999 my friends Peter and Verna Coleman were staying for a few days with my wife and me in our London flat. Verna had recently written a biography of the Australian poet and novelist Frederic Manning, author of *The Middle Parts of Fortune*, who had died in 1935.

Verna told me about the extensive research needed for the book, most of it done in England, where Manning lived after 1903. I asked if she had found many of his letters and if she was able to decipher his handwriting. Regretfully, she told me she had been disappointed not to have found a single letter from him, despite an exhaustive search.

The day following this conversation I had to go to a chemist's in Earls Court to collect a prescription for my son. Once I had done this I headed back towards the underground station, but something made me pause and look around. Some distance away, on the other side of the street, was an unappealing junk shop. I walked over to it and looked through the window. There was nothing much inside except broken kitchen goods: stoves, cupboards, et cetera. I was about to walk back to the underground when

I noticed a tin bucket on the floor from which some books protruded. I went into the store and put my hand into the bucket and pulled out a book.

It was a novel by Frederic Manning. A letter fell out of it. The letter was in Manning's handwriting and was a courteous reply, over two pages, to a man who had written to him asking if a book of his was to be reprinted.

That evening I handed the letter, and the book, to an astonished Verna, who thought I must have spent the day engaged in some skilled sleuthing.

...

Another book story is slightly similar. After my friend Barry Humphries' marriage to his wife Diane broke up, the enraged Diane cut up a number of his suits with scissors (a favourite pastime of bitter wives) and disposed of a number of volumes of Barry's collection of rare books. Barry mentioned to me one day that he particularly regretted the loss of a book by his old friend the arts writer Julian Jebb, a grandson of Hilaire Belloc. Julian had died in 1984. The book had contained a letter to Barry from Julian.

A few weeks after this conversation I was at the flea market in Rozelle, Sydney, where I often found copies of my own films, invariably for sale at embarrassingly low prices. (I buy these not for self-aggrandisement but because I am often asked for copies by people who assume I must have a stockpile that I am only too happy to share.) I noticed a huge pile of books that had been dumped on the ground in the shape of a collapsed pyramid. Trancelike, I walked over to the pile, plunged my hand in and pulled out one book. It was Barry's book by Julian Jebb, complete with the letter still neatly folded inside the front cover.

...

My final anecdote is without a satisfying finale, but is often in my thoughts. In 1968 I was photographing a film for a young director named Richard Saunders. We had to drive each day out to Berkhamsted to film in a small forest outside the town. Berkhamsted is quite a pretty commuter town about twenty-five miles from London, most notable for being the birthplace of Graham Greene.

Throughout the town there were a lot of notices stuck on fences and telegraph poles about the murder of two small boys, with a warning that the killer could be a local, so care should be taken, children not left unattended and so on.

Usually we drove back to London each evening after the filming but one Saturday I noticed that the elderly man acting in the film—there was a cast of two, the other being an attractive German girl—was exhausted. I suggested we find a bed and breakfast for him so he could rest. We would pick him up on Sunday morning.

A small, neat house not far away had a B&B sign

displayed. I went to the door, followed by the old actor and Richard Saunders. A middle-aged couple came to the door. I took one look at the man and immediately became nauseated. I looked at him in horror as his wife told us the charge would be one pound for the night. He seemed to radiate evil. I said nothing, but quickly hustled everyone away and back to the car.

Baffled by the change of plans, the others demanded to know what the problem was. I couldn't tell them that I felt the man at the door was the killer of the children. I knew it would sound absurd. Probably it was. I just said it would be more sensible to drive back to London as we usually did.

...

Richard Saunders' filmmaking career went nowhere, despite some promising short films. He had little organisational skill and couldn't deal with associates with any grace, both useful attributes for filmmaking.

I never found out if anyone was arrested for the child murders in Berkhamsted.

2017

II

Making and Not Making Movies

Stumbling Towards Directing

I grew up in the suburbs west of Sydney in perhaps the most boring decade in Australia's history: the 1950s. At first we—mother, father, sister and myself—were in a fibro house in unfashionable Toongabbie. Fibro, which is asbestos, is so fragile that it was quite easy to bump against a wall and knock a hole right through it. A further oddity was that the designers had forgotten to include a kitchen, so at the last moment put a stove and sink in the lounge room. There was no refrigeration. I have a vivid memory of a man wearing shorts running down the side of the house in the early morning with a large ice block he held in pincers. He dropped the block into the ice box outside the back door, then ran back to his truck to grab a block for the next house.

After some years there we moved a couple of miles to a slightly more stylish house in Wentworthville. This house had the disadvantage of being opposite a Baptist church, which had services all day Saturday. My father was persuaded to join the congregation, and my sister and I were expected to attend the interminable all-day sessions. Following one or two of these I resisted firmly, refusing to attend despite the pleas of the earnest minister, an American, and his sidekick, an even more earnest Australian.

At least there were 'picture shows' around then: one in almost every little town, all the way west from Parramatta to Penrith. Most were fairly ramshackle church halls or decrepit wooden buildings with a School of Arts sign over the door. We didn't use the words 'movies' or 'cinema'. We were 'going to the pictures'. My parents didn't really approve of my going, though were vague about the reasons. My mother had delusions of grandeur and considered films to be for 'the lower classes'—she seemed quite unaware that we qualified, or very nearly qualified, as members of this group.

I wanted to make films from the time I saw my first films in the mid-1940s. Unlike my school friends I had no interest in animated films (I still don't) but was fascinated by narratives with actors. Somehow I realised, while still very young, that the key person in all the films was not the dashing leading man or beautiful heroine, but the director. I admired certain directors and avidly followed their work. Film directors have distinctive styles just as painters do. Among my favourites were Howard Hawks, John Ford, William Wyler, Carol Reed and quite a number of lesser names, many of whom directed B westerns or action films—names like Budd Boetticher, John Sturges, Anthony Mann and Jacques Tourneur. It would be some years before I found out that films were made in languages other than English.

By the time I was around twelve my mother had given up trying to sabotage my film-going and accepted that I could go once a week. Years later, when I had directed some films in Los Angeles and brought back tape copies to show her, I realised she'd seen so few films in her life that she found them totally confusing because she had never learnt the language of film. A change of scene she often found baffling. 'You've made a mistake,' she said to me at one point during a screening of *Crimes of the Heart* (1986). 'That man is wearing the wrong coat.' She couldn't accept my explanation that it was a different day and he'd changed his wardrobe. She did not have the patience to try to follow plots, while flashbacks were bewildering and incomprehensible.

It always took a huge effort to get my father to drive me to distant suburban picture palaces so I could catch some major revival. He had enthused for years over John Ford's *My Darling Clementine* (1946)—despite the absence of the two stars he liked, Ronald Colman and Errol Flynn—and agreed to take me to it one night in 1954, when it was shown at a theatre in Newtown. I think somehow his befuddled thought processes caused him to identify with the silent, tough but undemonstrative Wyatt Earp in Henry Fonda's subtle performance.

I shared his enthusiasm for *Clementine*. It seemed to me, and still seems to me, an almost perfect film, despite the producer Darryl Zanuck's re-editing of sections and his disastrous idea of adding close-ups of Fonda in the middle of Ford's delicate and effective ending. Flawlessly directed by Ford and mercifully free of his often ineptly broad comic scenes, its strong story is tightly scripted and superbly acted by Fonda, Victor Mature, Walter Brennan and Linda Darnell. It confirmed my ambition to be a film director—an ambition that seemed ridiculous in Australia at that time, when years would go by with no locally made films at all. Australians even seemed ashamed of their accents; all the newsreaders were English, or Australians affecting an English accent.

At university I joined the University Players, mainly because that was where all the prettiest girls seemed to be. As an actor I was ineffectual and overwhelmed by a number of gifted performers, including John Bell, Arthur Dignam, Andrew McLennan, Vashti Farrar, Anne Schofield and

John Gaden. One weekend I volunteered for set painting, under the impression that some of the girls would be there, too. There weren't any, but the director of the play, Ken Horler, had brought along a record player. I was stunned at the sound of the first disc he put on; I'd never heard anything so exciting. It was Bartók's *Concerto for Orchestra* and it introduced me to classical music all at one blow. I was eighteen and knew little about music, owing to my father's hatred of noise of any kind and his strict rules governing behaviour in our household.

...

When I graduated I went straight to England, travelling in an Italian ship, the *Castel Felice*. I shared a cabin below the waterline with five other men.

My film career progressed slowly. I didn't know that in England the unions in those days had a policy called 'closed shop'. This meant they wouldn't let anyone into the film industry (and other industries) until all the current members were employed. This was never going to happen, so the industry was moribund. The union, the ACTT, had an office in Soho Square, in an elegant building that was once the Venetian Embassy. I naively knocked on the door, which didn't open, but a face appeared when a metal slot was slid back. I was curtly asked what I wanted and replied that I wanted to join the film union. I was given what was clearly a standard reply: 'You can't join without having a job in the film business and you can't get a job without being a union member.' My attempt to discuss this conundrum was cut short when the metal grille snapped shut.

The much reviled Mrs Thatcher later outlawed closed shops when she became prime minister and film production in Britain revived almost immediately.

With my limited funds from Australia about to run out, I went to a labour exchange and found a job for some months at a place called Cornwall's Erections. The job consisted of dismantling a factory that was being moved out of London. The work was so exhausting and so dirty that when I returned to my shared apartment each day my roommates, Clive James and Michael Newman, threw me into the bath and scrubbed me. At least, this was their initial reaction. They soon tired of it.

After the factory was demolished, I did a few harrowing months as the only male teacher at a girls' secondary school in Willesden. The intense scrutiny of hundreds of young women was debilitating. Then, on the back page of *The Times*, I saw a job advertised as a film editor in Nigeria (a country I couldn't place with accuracy, though I knew it was in Africa) and applied for that. At least it was film work. I found out I was the only applicant—not one of those out-of-work English film technicians thought it was worthwhile.

I stayed in Enugu, the capital of Eastern Nigeria, for two years. The film unit made no films at all but I kept myself busy by joining a local theatre group of African actors. I directed plays with them and appeared as the missionary in a couple of plays by Nigerian writers. When I came on stage the audience would boo me, in a good-natured sort of way, as missionaries were no longer highly regarded. However, I noticed that all of the Nigerians who spoke flawless English, with a large vocabulary, had been educated at schools run by Irish Catholic priests.

With the Biafran War about to begin, I caught a very slow train to Port Harcourt, then found a cargo ship on which I could get a berth back to England. The Biafran War turned out to be a tragic affair in which a number of my Nigerian friends were killed.

Back in England in 1965 I applied for a job with the British Film Institute, which had a modest fund, the Production Board, to help filmmakers get started—and it was non-union. I've no idea why I was selected; perhaps it was my enthusiastic letter of application, along with my Sydney University degree and the fact I'd made a couple of short films. When I was interviewed by a gaggle of knights and one or two lords I thought my chances were zero and the job would go to an Oxbridge graduate. I was surprised when the director of the BFI, Stanley Reed, said, 'We are interested in you for this position, Bruce.'

I stayed at the BFI for about five years. The chairman of the Production Board was the delightful Sir Michael Balcon, founder of the famous Ealing Studios. Board members came and went over the years but were always an interesting cross-section of the arts—film directors such as Karel Reisz and Lindsay Anderson; an art critic, David Sylvester; a couple of academics whose names I've forgotten; a celebrated documentary filmmaker, Basil Wright; a Royal Court Theatre director, William Gaskill; and an intellectual film critic, Eric Rhode. Most were friendly and straightforward and very interested in the work of up-and-coming filmmakers. Still, it took me some time to call Lord Elton 'Arthur', as he insisted.

My job was to meet all of the applicants to the board and, in effect, do a feasibility study of their projects. Could the BFI afford to make the script in question? Was it too ambitious for novice filmmakers? And so on. During my time at the BFI many important careers began, including those of Ridley and Tony Scott, Stephen Frears, Mike Leigh, B. S. Johnson, Don Levy and Nick Broomfield.

Somehow, I also found myself on the board of the Arts Council, as 'film advisor'. This board was equally distinguished. It included the painters Sir Lawrence Gowing (chairman—though he had a stutter he described as 'the best in England') and Sir William Coldstream, the writer V. S. Naipaul, and the painter and art collector Sir Roland Penrose. Between 1966 and 1972 I was involved in the production of documentaries about Picasso's sculpture, Indian Village art, Poussin, Lichtenstein, Barbara Hepworth, Henry Moore, Giacometti and Magritte.

...

By now I had become obsessed by classical music but knew very little about opera. I'd seen one or two productions at the Elizabethan Theatre in Newtown near the university before I left for England, but they were shoddily produced, if well sung, and the stories seemed downright silly. Of course, virtually all of the great nineteenth-century operas have monumentally inane stories adapted from popular plays or novels of the period—though this doesn't stop some of them, I realised eventually, from being masterpieces. Emotional music papered over the improbable plots. Poetic lyrics negated melodramatic and/or sentimental situations.

My conversion to opera came as suddenly as the Bartók incident. In 1966 a university friend, John Stoddart, invited me to his house in Notting Hill Gate to watch a BBC telecast of Benjamin Britten's *Peter Grimes.* I turned up thinking there would be free food and some attractive girls, though I'd be bored with the opera. The food was good, there were no girls at all, but the opera was stunning. I later saw the same version on stage, with the same tenor, the Canadian Jon Vickers—still in my opinion the greatest Grimes ever. The story, of a tormented Norfolk fisherman, was so moving I found myself in tears almost throughout.

I've seen at least a dozen productions of the opera over the years and it always moves me, even in relatively indifferent productions. The libretto rounds out a number of characters and the music, ceaselessly melodic, seems to penetrate their souls. Perhaps not just theirs, but those of the audience as well. A few years ago I was at a dinner party in London where one of the guests was the Australian conductor Sir Charles Mackerras. I heard a lady at the far end of the table say, 'Sir Charles, what do you consider to be the greatest opera ever written?' Without a pause, he said, '*Peter Grimes*, without a doubt.'

By now I was an opera fanatic. I remember spending five pounds going to see Britten's *Billy Budd* in London when my salary, teaching at the girls' school, was twelve pounds a week.

In 1972, encouraged by news of government investment in the Australian film industry, I returned to Sydney and, with the assistance of Phillip Adams, made my first feature, *The Adventures of Barry McKenzie*, which Barry Humphries and I had adapted from his scurrilous *Private Eye* comic strip. Despite its popular success it was a critical disaster and I returned to England to see what work I could find.

I was rescued by Phillip Adams and David Williamson, who called and asked if I'd be interested in making a film of David's play *Don's Party*. I returned to Australia almost immediately. *Don's Party* (1976) gave me a degree of critical credibility—much more important than commercial success, I realised. This was followed by *The Getting of Wisdom* (1978), *Breaker Morant* and *Puberty Blues* (1981). As I write this, in 2017, I have just finished shooting my thirty-second film, in Toronto.

I never thought of directing an opera until I met the Italian-American composer Gian Carlo Menotti in Spoleto, South Carolina, in 1985. He asked if I was the 'film director interested in opera', then went on to suggest I direct one for the Spoleto Festival. I told him I had no musical training and couldn't read music, despite strenuous efforts to do so (similar to my efforts to learn French and Spanish). He pointed out that I was directing the opera, not conducting it. So…

I thought, it's probably like directing a film, except that the audience watches everything in wide shot without cutting—this would give me the exciting challenge of making the drama work within those parameters. Of course, the music would be a great help.

Since *The Girl of the Golden West* at Spoleto I have directed *The Crucible*, *Rigoletto*, *Sweeney Todd* and *Cold Sassy Tree*. In Australia I directed the Australian premieres of *A Streetcar Named Desire* (André Previn), *The Dead City* (Erich Korngold), *Elektra* (Richard Strauss) and *Of Mice and Men* (Carlisle Floyd).

In Brisbane in 2016 I directed Britten's comic opera *Albert Herring*. His *Peter Grimes* continues to elude me; it's always being handed to other directors. But I feel I'm stumbling towards it.

2017

A Career of Sorts

After I directed my first feature film, *The Adventures of Barry McKenzie*, in Australia in 1972 I made a number of others through the 1970s. My greatest success in that period was *Breaker Morant* in 1979. This film was shown at Cannes in 1980 and led to a number of offers from Hollywood. I selected a very low-budget film called *Tender Mercies*, written by the wonderful Horton Foote, who had written a number of plays for both stage and television that invariably dealt with aspects of rural life (the Texas where he grew up) with insight and compassion. The film was no box-office smash but I was nominated for an Academy Award as Best Director (I'd already been nominated for my screenplay of *Breaker Morant*).

My Hollywood career continued through the 1980s, interspersed with films in Europe and Australia, culminating in *Driving Miss Daisy* winning the Academy Award for Best Picture in 1990. I didn't win Best Director, as I wasn't nominated. (Only a couple of times in the history of the Academy Awards has a film been a contender for Best Picture but the director not nominated.)

Looking back after many more films, I think directors had an easier task in realising their concepts prior to, broadly speaking, the year 2000. Up until then everything was shot on film and the rushes or dailies were screened a day or two later to a small group—usually just the director and cameraman, and possibly the producer and one or two cast members.

Studio executives, financiers, sales agents, distributors and suchlike had little or no access to the material. Certainly, various people at the financing studio saw footage from time to time but this was invariably in the form of uncut and ungraded rushes. They could, and did, make comments about what they were seeing; there have been many celebrated cases, since at least 1910, of films being stopped, reshot, recast and so on; but in general there was not the micromanaging characteristic of filmmaking today.

The situation is somewhat different now, for a number of reasons.

First, the introduction of digital filmmaking means that virtually everyone connected with a film, and all too many not connected, can instantly be given copies on disc or simply by email of all the filmed material. It's very easy to view this material at home or an office desk, which means that snap judgments can be made by a large number of backroom meddlers. Further, the more technical of them can edit the scenes themselves on their own computers. It's then a simple matter to get in touch with the director, on set or on location, and inundate him with comments about what he's shot, along with advice on how to improve it. These people will frequently also give the director the immense benefit of their insights on performances, sound recording and photography.

Even on set the situation has deteriorated for the director. At one time the director had to look through the camera or a viewfinder and then discuss the shot with the cameraman. Now, with digital technology, screens are everywhere—displaying the image that is currently being photographed. Quite often the director himself is not even on the set but in a tent with a screen—a big mistake, in my view, as it alienates him from his all-important relationship with the actors. Worst of all, video screens sprout up like fungi all around the back of the set, where they are viewed by an ever increasing band of people who have some connection, often a tenuous one, with the film. This connection is usually financial, rarely creative.

Often one or other of them rushes to the set to confer with the director, or calls the director away from the set for a meeting. They can then make some complaint, invariably referred to as an 'observation' and labelled 'sharing our thoughts', about some aspect of the production. This could be an actor's performance, a camera angle, an aspect of the lighting or any of a number of other factors which would be best left to the director to decide. The director can waste valuable directing time explaining politely what it is he's doing and why he's doing it, or can lose his temper and expel the entire entourage from the set. This tends to work only in the short term as, like termites after a visit from pest controllers, they usually manage to re-insinuate themselves, if not on the set itself then from nearby hotel rooms where they continue viewing the progress of the film on their computers.

I know, of course, that a lot of money is being spent on even a low-budget film and financiers are understandably apprehensive. All the same it, is by far the best policy, once a director has been chosen, to let him get on and actually direct the film without second-guessing his choices. The director should have, and most *do* have, an image of the completed film in their head. They are working towards this through the complicated process of realisation—shooting, guiding performances, editing, mixing the sound and grading the image.

Almost inevitably, those people watching the work in progress, which is almost never filmed in sequence, have no such concept. They are reacting to moments of the film, never realising that the director is building an edifice stone by stone and only he knows the correct position for each one. I am not saying that all directors are gifted; many lack talent and some are quite mad; but the vast majority are talented artists and it's best if the final film includes only their mistakes rather than the mistakes of well-meaning onlookers, most of whom are doing no more than trying unconvincingly to justify their jobs.

I am not saying that the director must be given carte blanche. Once the film has been edited into a first cut most directors welcome input from others, even viewers chosen at random. Usually, in fact, these are the ones best positioned to give advice, as they want simply to be entertained. They have no vested interest in the production.

Executives of production companies can also be quite astute although, once again, many of them make decisions based not simply on the film itself but on some vague image they have of what they imagine the market will accept. Advice at this stage—after early cuts of the film—is the most perilous for the director. Definitely nervous breakdown territory, as he realises that he frequently has to deal with changes he suspects will destroy his movie. The more enlightened production executives present their 'notes' as 'suggestions' which the director can consider—then adopt the ones he agrees with and discard the remainder. But—all too often these days, because of tension over financial pressures and the input of distributors and sales agents—the 'notes' are not suggestions but directives, resulting in a situation where the director has the depressing task of supervising changes he believes will be to the film's detriment, not its advantage.

I must say this has happened to me only once or twice and I've been lucky to work with producers as enlightened as Richard Zanuck on *Driving Miss Daisy*, Barry Spikings and John Cohn on *Tender Mercies*, Sue Milliken on *Black Robe* (1991), and the legendary Dino De Laurentiis on *Crimes of the Heart*. All of these people were not hesitant in giving their views on the progress of the film as it proceeded towards a final cut (which can take six months or more) but never forced changes that I thought were mistaken.

...

I have been writing about the characteristics of actually shooting and editing a film these days, but setting them up in the first place has also changed considerably in the past ten years.

The market has broadened considerably as a result of DVDs and instant accessibility through television, Netflix, computers and iPads. The actual cinema-going group is perceived to be, and is, mostly in the fifteen-to-twenty-six age bracket, and a lot of formulaic action films and, curiously, zombie movies are made because of the peculiar belief that this age group wants little else. Broadly speaking, as there are always exceptions, production has split into two sections: big-budget studio films, almost all either action movies or teen comedies, and low-budget 'quality' films aimed at a more discriminating market. I'm excluding material made predominantly for television. The standard of this has gone up in recent years as the best writers have found a shrunken market for their work in the world of feature films and can now take credit for the generally high standard of mini-series and films made for television.

For the director, setting up a low-budget film—say, under $15 million—can be a heartbreaking undertaking. Almost always, no one group will supply the finance. It may be a combination of money from a private investor, a contribution from a studio's 'art-house' film division, perhaps the government of a state or even a country somewhere offering a rebate which is a percentage of money spent, a loan from a bank or investment firm (at an iniquitous interest rate) and a contribution from a sales agent against projected revenue of the final film.

Putting all of this lot together would tax the organisational skill of whoever planned the D-Day landings. Virtually all of these groups will have comments to make about the script. This is hardly surprising, but the majority of them are inept as critics and shackled by their adherence to the characteristics of previous films which proved financially successful, which explains why films as superbly written as *The King's Speech* (2010) took many years to find backers.

Richard Zanuck and I spent some years looking for finance for *Driving Miss Daisy* and were constantly assured by readers—mostly young college graduates who read for the executives who are too lazy to read for themselves—that the script was not worth filming. (Among its Academy Awards was one for Best Screenplay.) One day, in despair, I remember saying to Zanuck, 'All these people who tell us the script is worthless—can they all be wrong and the two of us be right?' He replied, calmly, 'Yes, that is the case.'

A producer friend of mine in Los Angeles recently produced a comedy set in a ski resort. When I saw the film I commented to him that it was disappointing and asked how he—and I knew he had excellent taste—managed to get mixed up with such a tenth-rate film. Wearily, he replied, 'If you'd read the original script you'd have seen why I was so enthusiastic.' Like so many films, it was altered as a result of disastrous input from various groups who put in finance under certain conditions.

For the director, one of the more depressing aspects of production these days is the rise of the sales agents, who to a large extent have supplanted casting directors. Sales agents not only comment on the scripts, with varying degrees of perspicacity, but are all too often asked by the producers which actors should be cast in order to be able to find the finance to make the film. They then supply a list of names, rated in order of preference. Little attention is paid to suitability for the roles under discussion, which accounts for the numerous examples of miscasting in so many current films.

I've noticed that it's a characteristic of these sales agents that although they may know who is currently popular—not exactly a difficult assessment—they are notoriously bad at pinpointing the up-and-coming stars. In my own experience, over the years I've had rejected—just before international fame struck them—Daniel Day-Lewis, Hugh Grant, Alan Cumming, Cate Blanchett, Morgan Freeman, Julianna Margulies, Chris Cooper, Queen Latifah, Judy Davis, Sarah Jessica Parker, Helena Bonham Carter and Michael Fassbender.

Actors' agents are frequently also a nightmare for the director. Many of the large agencies represent a roster of star names and do their best to ensure that financed or could-be-financed scripts under their control are cast entirely by actors on their books. It is possible for directors to press for actors from other agencies but this is discouraged, no matter how suitable the actor may be for the role in question. If the fees involved threaten to be modest, the agencies often show no interest whatever in casting anyone at all.

When *Driving Miss Daisy* was in preparation, the studio (Warners, although they had only a minor part of the financial investment) insisted on a name actor to play

Miss Daisy's son, as neither Morgan Freeman nor Jessica Tandy was widely known at that time. (Morgan had made only one previous film and Jessica was predominantly a stage actress, so unknown in Los Angeles.) Every agency in Los Angeles reported that no one was interested in the part. Richard and Lili Zanuck, the producers, were on the point of abandoning the film. I was preparing to return to Australia when I had a phone call from Dan Ackroyd, offering to play the role. Evidently someone had told him, at a party, that we were desperate. He'd probably seen the Off-Broadway stage play on which the film was based. He took the role of Boolie for the trifling fee we could afford and received an Academy Award nomination for his performance.

Ever since the beginnings of the film industry changes have been made to films by distributors. Celebrated cases include the drastic abbreviation of Visconti's masterpiece *Rocco and His Brothers* (1960) in America and the weird alterations made to Ridley Scott's superb *Blade Runner* (1982). The director's cuts of these films available on DVD show the superiority of the director's vision. Now, unfortunately, it is easier than ever technically to alter films and distributors have reacted to this with enthusiasm. Directors' guilds and unions will attempt to preserve the director's vision, but the alternative often presented is of no distribution at all—if the director doesn't agree to changes.

Even worse, a director may imagine he has the final

cut but a cleverly worded clause in his contract may give this right to the distributor, who can then recut and remix with abandon. His intention, of course, is to broaden the appeal of the film—but, as the film has not at this stage been released, he is simply guessing that his changes will be to the film's advantage. Interestingly, a number of distributors and film executives, blinded by the ease with which they changed other directors' films, have turned director themselves. The results have invariably been disastrous, I am happy to report.

Despite all these difficulties, many fine films are made all over the world; there are great directors in every country, dedicated to their art and imbued with the spirit that conquers every obstacle.

2012

Thoughts about Actors and Acting

An ability to dive in and out of other people's lives and emotions is important for an actor. Can an actor actually truly *be* that other person? Well, momentarily, they can inhabit that person completely. They switch into it and I'm often aware when I'm directing them that they are, basically, someone else. And I find it's only if I believe that they are someone else that the role they are playing will be convincing. At the same time, it's worth pointing out that many actors have become world-famous without being even remotely convincing. They give essentially the same performance in role after role but might have a physical appearance that is much admired and/or a degree of charm that propels them from film to film. I'm not denigrating those performers. Who could resist the appeal of, say, Errol Flynn?

Film acting isn't as straightforward as it may appear to be. True, actors in films rarely have to learn a couple of hours of dialogue and perform it without a break, as they would in a play. In fact, in films a take of even one minute would be considered quite long, but there are quite a few variables to master. Film actors are required to move at a certain moment to a precise spot, where even an error of a couple of inches can necessitate a retake. They could now have moved out of the area that was lit for them or could be in a position where they block or fail to reveal other cast members. And so on.

As a director I'm always meticulous about composition and lighting. With me, and with other directors who I believe work like I do, actors have to deal with two basics: *Not only do I have to do this emotional scene, but he wants me to be at that mark on the carpet on a certain word!* And somehow they've got to get both things happening together. Invariably they do. Or most of them do. Occasionally I've worked with actors who oddly resent the filmmaking process—even though they are receiving a huge fee to participate in it. They want to work as if they are on stage, where their movements are much less precise.

Some directors, I'm told (I have never been on a film set with another director so have never seen one in action), work in a much freer style. They'll just set the camera and say to the actors, 'Move wherever you like.' Then the actors don't have to worry about the technical aspects of the scene. When they are allowed to do that it's a bit easier for them to concentrate on their acting—they don't have to worry about being in certain positions for the camera. But I prefer to be in control of all the variables, so that I know exactly what I'm getting and how it's going to be edited—because, on film, the final emotional effect is a combination of a number of factors. It's not just a matter of photographing people talking. It's the way the camera *perceives* them acting, the lens that is being used, the lighting of the scene, the depth of focus and the editing pattern.

All of these factors combine to have an emotional effect on the audience. So I don't want my actors to move wherever they like—I want to be the one to choreograph all the moves. John Ford, Orson Welles, Martin Scorsese, Jean Renoir, Ingmar Bergman, Michael Haneke and Carol Reed have produced work that could not possibly have been directed by anyone else, and they do (or did) this by having a vision of their own. The actors are a part of this vision. Perhaps a key part, but a part.

Some of the actors I have worked with are able to switch in and out of the character they are playing with startling ease. English actors, in particular, are mostly able to do this, probably because of their intensive stage training. I've worked with English actors who will be in the middle of telling a joke, which I interrupt with a call of 'action'. With no hesitation they will go straight into an emotional scene, complete with tears. After 'cut' is called they calmly return to their joke. Most American actors (and certainly some English and Australian ones) can't do that. They will closet themselves away and try to be the character all the time, a few even going to the extent of insisting on being addressed by the name of the person they are playing at all times, which can lead to moments of hilarity. 'Mr Lincoln, it's time for our lunch break'; 'Hamlet, are you ready to return to your luxury hotel?'

Quite often the sheer technical skill of actors amazes me. When I was directing Sharon Stone I had a complicated tracking shot planned and said to her, 'It'd be great if, just as the camera passes you, you begin to cry.' She replied, 'Do you want tears in both eyes or just one eye?' I thought she was joking, but I said, 'Can it be just one eye?' She said, 'Yes. Which one would be better for the light, the left or right?' Dubious about all this, I told her the left eye would be preferable. 'Where will the camera be when you want the tear to roll?'—so I marked a point for her and then watched with astonishment as the tear rolled at exactly the marked point for five takes.

And yet...perhaps it wasn't all that difficult. I've noticed that women actors ('actresses' is no longer de rigueur) can usually cry without any help from the make-up department. Men usually need the help of fake tears, although I remember filming a scene with Jonathan Pryce in a film about Alma Mahler (*Bride of the Wind*, 2001) and his tears were so affecting that I felt, standing by the camera a few feet away from him, that I had no right to intrude on some profoundly personal emotion that was being used to give me the scene I wanted.

...

I'm often asked what I'm looking for at auditions. A key factor, which I know a lot of actors resent, is that their physical appearance fits, to some extent, my conception of the character they may be asked to impersonate. Perhaps more importantly, as they read pages from the script I'm looking for their insight, their attitude towards the role. If they read the lines and I think the emotional nuances are all topsy-turvy, I don't bother with them. But if their instincts about the role are similar to mine, then it's much more likely I'll cast them. I could be wrong, of course, but that's beside the point. I'm the director.

I don't usually talk to them much about the role before they read. But I sometimes do, and if they ask questions about it I'll answer them. But it's their take on it that I'm interested in. I avoid discussions because I don't want them to give me something that they think I want.

Sometimes an actor will read perfectly competently and I could still think their interpretation is totally wrong, at least according to my conception of the part. At other times people have come and read not particularly well but I've thought they have enormous potential, so I've still cast them, often despite the objections of producers or finance people who view the audition tapes and don't agree with my assessments.

The famous stage director Tyrone Guthrie was once asked how he always elicited wonderful performances from the actors in the plays he directed. He replied, 'Casting, dear boy, casting.' With the right actor in the role the film or play will invariably proceed smoothly. It can quickly become hell for the director if the wrong person is in the role—something that often happens if an actor is cast because of their name value or because of some whim by the film's financiers.

Luckily, there are a few subterfuges available to the director, all designed to minimise the impact of the miscast actor. He or she can be filmed in wide shots so that their inept performance will not have the impact of a close-up, he/she can be placed in shadows (for the same reason), and the performance can be edited in such a way that other actors are favoured and the offender will be seen mostly from behind and/or have chunks of their dialogue removed. Revoicing a performance with another actor is a difficult option, as the actors' guilds usually forbid this by contract.

But each of these devices can certainly help, although they may not go all the way into saving the film.

Subterfuges have led to some amazing incidents. The distinguished producer David Puttnam told me that he removed a lead actress entirely from a film (it was *Chariots of Fire*, 1981), although he was quick to point out it wasn't a performance issue but was done in the interests of simplifying the plotline. He added that he never quite summed up the courage to tell the young lady what he'd done and was stunned to see her at the London premiere of the film. Not surprisingly, she never spoke to him again.

...

People not working in the film industry seem to have the idea that many actors are difficult to work with; this is to be expected, given that media stories are often recounted of on-set tantrums and 'creative differences', which sometimes involve brawls, a number of which manage to find their way onto the internet. I've encountered very few of these. One young lady in a recent film of mine made little effort to remember her lines and lost us two days of the shooting schedule, and another celebrated (male) actor had no trouble with his lines but was intent on creating a hostile atmosphere with his fellow performers, which led to an on-set scuffle. But there is no doubt that the vast majority of actors are hard-working and co-operative.

There seems to be a general feeling that really famous actors are more difficult to direct, or resist direction. It is true that I've met one or two (in over thirty films!) who regard the director as an opponent, but the vast majority of celebrity actors I've directed are involved and inventive, with a willingness to make my ideas for the scene actually work.

I expect actors to make suggestions as we film the scenes. I can't think of everything and I'm not acting the roles, so I appreciate actors coming to me to say something like, 'I've been having a think about the scene, and I thought maybe I could do this at this moment?' However, it is important to me as a director that the decision about whether we adopt the suggestion or not is mine. So I might say, 'Yes, I think that's a good idea. Let's do it, and I'll cover it this way.' But sometimes I might say, 'It won't work—we're not going to do it,' and at that point I expect them to say, 'Okay, well, we won't do it. We'll do it your way.' Usually, they do, although once or twice I've had some problems.

I was directing Jessica Lange in *Crimes of the Heart* and she wanted to play a scene rather differently to the way I had outlined it. She's a terrific actor, but very strong-willed. So I said, 'Jessica, you want to direct, don't you?' She replied, 'Yes, I do. I'm going to direct a film.' And I said, 'That's wonderful. Now, when you're directing and an actor comes up to you and says to you that there's something he wants to do, and it's contrary to what you want, you will, of course, let him do exactly what he wants, won't you?' And she looked at me blankly and just walked away…and did the scene in the way I wanted.

But I usually find, having worked with a lot of huge stars in America, that they tend to be accommodating and skilled. The reason they're huge stars is largely because of their technical skills, ability to co-operate and, often, sheer charisma. I recently directed a film with the actress-singer Queen Latifah. I thought she was very good as we shot the film, but when I viewed the material in the editing room I realised she was one of those actors whose magic is more apparent in the finished film. The camera seems to discover something indefinable, something extra.

I had the same experience when Cate Blanchett first auditioned for me, for a role in *Paradise Road* (1997). I thought she was wonderful at the reading in the casting director's studio, but when I watched the audition tape that night she was even more compelling. I phoned my agent in Los Angeles and told him I'd found a young woman who had such talent she was going to be a huge star within a couple of years. I urged him to represent her in America. He ignored me, to his cost, as she quickly won a couple of Academy Awards and played leading roles in numerous major films.

…

It surprises me how often there are roles in films that nobody wants to play—roles that strike me as appealing, with good dialogue and strong situations. This invariably baffles me. Some years ago I had a film I wanted to do in Australia, *Our Country's Good*, from the 1988 play by Timberlake Wertenbaker, a wonderful writer. She adapted the play and film script from the Thomas Keneally novel *The Playmaker* (1987). The producer was the dynamic Ismail Merchant, who had produced a string of successes (including *The Remains of the Day*, 1993, and *A Room with a View*, 1985), most of them directed by James Ivory. *Our Country's Good* was all financed, all ready to go—but nobody wanted to be in it. Unbelievable. We couldn't find an actor.

Ismail and I spent two years trying to get a cast. We never managed to meet with even one actor. Not one! Finally, we quit. I said to him one day, 'We're going to have to give up on this.' He agreed, saying, 'It must be your fault. I've had no trouble finding actors for all my other films.' Luckily, my Los Angeles agent saved me from poverty by finding me a Hollywood film to direct, *Double Jeopardy* (1999). Every actor seemed to want to be in that one, yet I consider the project to be nowhere near the level of *Our Country's Good*.

When I saw Ismail in London a few years later we were still mystified. We had thought Australians in particular would fall over themselves to be in a strong story about the early years of the colony in New South Wales, but in fact they showed even less interest than English actors.

Some of my experiences have made me a little cynical when I hear actors complaining about the difficulty of finding work. When *Breaker Morant* was being prepared in 1979 two roles, Jack Thompson and Edward Woodward, were cast quite quickly. But the third role, of the young man who was on trial in the story, became a major problem. Nobody wanted to play it. The casting director, Alison Barrett, and I were completely stumped. I came up with the idea of going to the drama school NIDA, which I knew must have a lot of students around twenty years old—exactly the right age for the part.

I went and addressed all of the students. There in front of me was a great sea of young men. I told them about the film and gave them the address of the casting director and told them I'd be there Monday morning and to *please* just come along and audition. One person turned up: Lewis Fitz-Gerald. He gave an excellent reading of the script then said, 'Oh God, I hope I get it.' I said, 'Lewis, you have nothing to worry about. Nobody else has shown up.' He was flabbergasted. He said, 'Nobody came?! They were all talking about coming.' Why was Lewis the only actor interested in such a good role? I have no idea.

...

Drama schools these days, worldwide, are very thorough. They concentrate much more on the nuances of accents than was standard in the past. None of the actors in *Gone with the Wind* (1939), for example, made an attempt at a

Southern accent, apart from a half-hearted effort by Vivien Leigh in a few scenes. This would be unacceptable these days because the whole world has television and the internet, which familiarises audiences with global speech patterns. If actors don't hit the correct accent fairly accurately they will be ridiculed.

A couple of years ago I was auditioning some young actors in London. They would come into the casting office and invariably say, 'What's the accent?' And I'd say, 'Well, it's South London.' And they'd say, 'Which part?' Even, 'Which street?' Then they'd just do it. Some young Scottish actors auditioned. They talked so broadly in Scots that I found them hard to understand, but they could go straight into a South London dialect. Or speak with an upper-class accent. They'd leave and I'd say to the casting director, 'How accurate was the voice?' He'd say, 'Spot on.' Young actors in the United Kingdom are very good. But Australians can do it too. Just look at Cate Blanchett's various films. I cast a young Australian named Daniel Lapaine in *Double Jeopardy*. He came in to the audition and read with an American accent which was so convincing that my American film crew all assumed he was American.

When I did the film with Sharon Stone, *Last Dance* (1996), we had to revoice one young actor because when we previewed it someone came to me and said, 'Oh, I thought that character was supposed to be from West Tennessee?' And I said, 'Yes.' And they said, 'That accent's from East

Tennessee.' Well, I wouldn't know, of course, so I said to Sharon Stone, 'Has that comment about the accent got any validity?' She said, 'Yes, they're right—his accent's wrong. Just get him in and revoice it.' So I did: the same actor came in, happily admitting the original was from the wrong part of Tennessee.

...

When an actor is doing what they should be doing, they're interpreting someone else's life and bringing it to the rest of us with emotional truth; they're making it live, and they're doing it with emotional honesty. When Richard and Lili Zanuck were trying to set up *Driving Miss Daisy*, finance groups were virtually all of the opinion that no one would want to watch a film in which, essentially, three people are talking in a kitchen. They said, 'It just won't be interesting.' But Richard Zanuck maintained that it was so well written and had so much emotional truth in it that if it was well acted it could be commercially successful. He was right. We found the right cast, and it worked.

Emotions are a universal language. Everybody understands them. The way people feel is what we are trying to read in other people in real life all the time. We are, or most of us are, practised in the language of emotions. There's only a limited range of them and, of course, for all human beings they're all the same.

The only training I ever had in directing actors was when I was in Nigeria from 1964 to 1966 and was in a theatre company. In the role of a missionary in a white cassock I received a chorus of boos—not for my performance but because I represented a member of a group which had changed a way a life, and not for the better. I directed a few plays with all-African casts (including Pinter's *The Dumb Waiter*, 1957) and found the experience invaluable when I began directing feature films in Australia and, later, America.

I am rather suspicious of actors who go on and on to me about their roles. The more they tend to talk about finding this, finding that, the less I am confident that they really know what they're doing. Usually the more they analyse, the less confident and competent they are as actors. Almost always I find most of the actors who spend a lot of time trying to involve me in discussions about their characters are the ones who are the least gifted. They tend to produce a tedious load of theories about their character, and then play the role quite at variance with their own interpretation.

I remember Richard Dreyfuss (a very talented actor, but cerebral) bewildering me with impenetrable theories on how a scene we were about to film should be played. After listening for far too long I said, 'Richard, you play the scene and I'll tell you if I like it.' He looked rather taken aback at this idea but agreed to it. He was fine in the scene, as I knew he would be. No doubt he thought I was an intellectual lightweight, which I probably am, but he didn't bore me with his theories again.

Because of shooting schedules which mean movies are almost never filmed in sequence, it is crucial that actors have a thorough understanding of how their character arcs through the script. If they don't get that right, the characterisation could be uneven when the film is assembled, resulting in some terrible cutting and editing problems. So it's up to the actor, as well as the director, to make sure that that doesn't happen. A really astute actor will have a good understanding of where the pieces go together in the jigsaw, what emotional pitch they should strike in each scene.

The director is there, or should be there, to help hit the right tone, but I'm told a lot of directors just say to the actors, 'You're the actor—you act,' and concern themselves with camera angles and the pace of the film. Allegedly, the great American director William Wyler (*The Best Years of Our Lives*, *The Little Foxes*, *The Heiress*), who could even extract first-rate performances from the notoriously hammy Bette Davis, only ever said to his actors, 'Do it again, but better!' Actually, I'm not sure that this often-told story could be true.

I really get excited when an actor connects with emotional truth in a performance. But it should look simple and effortless. If an actor is too hyped up it's hard to watch them. (Emma Thompson always strikes me as overacting, even if she's sitting still listening to another actor speaking.)

I get very irritated. But when that emotional connection is really working I find it transporting. I have watched actors and become so involved in their character that I forget to call 'cut'. Then I'll catch an odd look from the crew or the actors themselves and call, 'Oh! Cut, cut, cut.' What they were doing was so good, so engaging that it just carried me away. And I'm pleased to say that happens a lot. The thing is, they have to believe in the character, know about the character, but then they have to do it simply. Don't try to do too much. Just try to be completely honest with it, and don't stress it. Just relax! The thing I most often say to actors is, 'Simpler, simpler, simpler. Do it simpler.'

I've heard it said that it's a good idea for actors to do nothing in their close-ups but to let audiences read something into the images. Often quoted in support of this (bizarre) belief is the final close-up of Greta Garbo in *Queen Christina* (1933), in which her expressionless face is held on screen for a long time. This always looked to me like an expressionless, blankly beautiful face, held on screen for a long time. Doing nothing results in nothing. In my opinion, the best procedure is for the actor to be thinking the right thoughts. The camera photographs thoughts, not just through expression in the eyes but through subtle body language. Greta Garbo was clearly thinking about nothing at all, perhaps only: 'How long is this shot going to be? I want to go home.'

The position of the camera, the number of people in the

shot, the depth of focus—is the background out of focus? Are other actors in focus in the same shot? These are all factors that affect performance, in which case the actor is more reliant on the director to tell him/her that some activity or expression should be stressed less or more because the audience is being bombarded with other stimuli. Actors are often surprised when I tell them to make something or other more emphatic, usually to a slight degree, when I had previously told them to make the same action less emphatic. It all depends on where the audience's attention is being directed.

People say that actors should know how to do this sort of thing, but I don't really think it's all that important. I suppose it's good for them to have some knowledge of these technical things, but in essence they just need to listen and trust. What's more important is that they trust the director—trust the director's eye.

And they need to be able to respond to a direction and adjust what they're doing straight away. Actors don't always know exactly how the camera is viewing the scene. These days, too, the director has to be cautious, as most scenes are filmed with two or three cameras (one camera was standard up until about twenty years ago), so the same action could be in a wide shot and close shot simultaneously.

In the close shot there is a danger of the acting seeming to be overplayed. The director's job has actually become more difficult as the number of cameras on the set increases.

Control, to some extent, is lost. It's impossible to watch a performance on three screens at the same time. All the more reason to cast carefully in the first place, so that an even tone can be maintained despite all the varied camera angles.

...

I don't know much about actor training because I've never been to any drama school. I don't actually know what they do in schools—but there are a lot of good actors around, so they must be doing something right.

Not all actors have been to drama schools, though many of them have learnt from stage performances, even amateur ones, television soap operas (where attractive looks are usually the key factor in selection for a role) or commercials. And there are certainly people, here and there, who seem able to slide into film acting and give unselfconscious performances just by instinct. I've cast a number of children who gave compelling performances with no acting training whatever. In fact, if they'd had some instruction from their parents it was invariably damaging, as the parents seem to favour Victorian melodramas and teach their children to overplay relentlessly. Finding children for roles can be a daunting task, usually involving auditioning numerous hopefuls. In my film *Evelyn* (2002), with Pierce Brosnan and Julianna Margulies, the young girl in the eponymous role, Sophie Vavasseur, was found after the casting director had auditioned over six hundred young ladies.

Unquestionably, drama schools are the best option for young people intent on an acting career. Questioning their value is pointless and naive, just as denigrating creative-writing courses is fruitless. Even Tennessee Williams did a creative-writing course at an American college. Acting is a complicated art, especially acting for film. Undoubtedly, a lot can be learnt from a course at a drama school. Let's face it, if you're going to be operated on by a surgeon, you'd rather he or she had been to a medical school.

2012

Financing Movies

This appears to be a boring topic, but the drama involved in raising finance for a film can be far more dramatic, even melodramatic, than the film itself.

Writers just need some paper and a pencil, or a computer, painters some canvas and paints, but film directors need millions of dollars of someone else's money. Finding this money can entangle the director and producer in years of effort, and failure is more common than success. A private income is desirable along the way to offset a total lack of earnings, but this seems to be quite rare. A struggle near the poverty line is more common, and is associated with the frequent break-up of relationships and marriages through stress.

For many years film production was dominated by the big studios whose trademarks we all know—the roaring lion of MGM, the searchlights of Fox, the mountain of Paramount, the lady with the ice cream on fire of Columbia Pictures, the radio tower on top of the globe of RKO (that was my favourite), the rotating globe of Universal International and, in England, the muscle man, Bombardier Billy Wells, hitting the gong of J. Arthur Rank. Shortly before he died a few years ago, Wells revealed that he never hit the gong at all. It was made of cardboard. The deep ringing sound was added later.

Some of these famous old studios still exist, though ownership has changed many times and now they're often just a branch, often a money-losing branch, of an even bigger conglomerate. Rupert Murdoch, for example, is the principal shareholder in 20th Century Fox. I've made films for Paramount, Fox, Warners and Disney, but now find myself more often looking for finance outside the studio system, where control of the film itself is more likely to remain in the hands of the director rather than a bunch of studio executives.

Even the major studios these days tend to look for financial partners for their productions, something they never did until comparatively recently. Costs have spiralled to the point where a film such as Michael Cimino's *Heaven's Gate* (1980) managed to put the oldest studio in Hollywood, United Artists, out of business, so it is considered prudent to spread the risk. There are successes, naturally, but it's not unusual to read of some film costing a couple of hundred million dollars and returning only a small percentage of the amount worldwide.

The reasons for the increased costs are complex—audiences are more demanding, so the films are constantly trying to outstrip one another with elaborate special effects. And advertising is a huge expense. It cost millions just to make people aware your movie exists.

But a key factor is the rise in power of actors. Actors in the old days of the 1920s through to the 1950s, even the 1960s, were under long-term contracts to the various studios and many of them spent their careers making film after film for the same studio. Salaries, by today's standards, were surprisingly modest. It took some time, a very long time it seems to me, for the actors and their agents to realise that in fact they held the whip hand all along. The public was really paying to go to see the big names. One by one the actors all gave up the studio contracts, went independent and negotiated fees film by film.

The power of the big stars grew around the globe, and these days a handful of them can command astronomical fees. Ten to twenty million dollars is not uncommon, plus a percentage of the profits, often the gross profits, which means they might get ten to fifteen per cent of the box office from the first dollar, with no deductions. Even the not-so-big names can rake in hundreds of thousands of dollars for a role—which usually involves only a couple of weeks' work.

No wonder I tried to persuade my children to become actors. I've failed with all four, which is depressing, as my numerous friends who decided to become professional actors have all done very well. Not all have become international superstars but all, despite their claims to the contrary, clearly have above-average incomes.

There are few directors who can get a gross percentage of the box office. They invariably have to make do with a net percentage. This means the percentage is paid after expenses such as print costs, advertising and so on are deducted. The result of all this is that it is rare for directors to realise any income at all from their percentage, no matter how successful the film. Numerous court cases have been fought over the issue, vast quantities of tears shed. A few years ago my agent called me about a film I was to direct for a major studio and told me, delightedly, that I was to receive fifteen per cent of the net profits. I told him I didn't want it, but would like one half of one per cent of the gross profits. He went back to the studio with this request—which was turned down.

These days, it's very difficult to set up a film without having a name actor attached, either through a studio or the independents. Without the name the finance will be withheld. An interesting corollary of this is the frequent disputes about who is and who is not a name actor. It can be argued that the chosen name for the role is in fact on a downward career path, or an unknown could be promoted with the claim that he or she is about to hit the big time. Often, I've found, the actor on the downward spiral was having only a temporary slump and the one about to hit the big time vanished without trace.

People often say to me: 'You've made so many films, you must be able to direct anything you want.' I wish that were the case. It might be true for Steven Spielberg or Peter Jackson, but not for me. Nor, I'm sure, for most directors.

To try to clarify this: a script *can* still be taken to one of the major studios. Despite everything, they have money and access to money, and if they green-light a project it has a good chance of going into production. (Not an absolute certainty, though. I've had a couple of films green-lit which still weren't made—probably because of a night of the long knives among the studio executives, which meant the new power-wielders scuttled the projects approved by their predecessors.) Even if a big-name actor is attached to a project the attachment could end at any time, as it is rarely a legal commitment. The star could abandon the film if a more lucrative or appealing offer is brought to him or her.

Further, even if the actor *is* attached and gives no sign of jumping ship, the director often enters into what is known as development hell. This means he is going to be inundated with script notes from the studio executives. These are usually hundreds of pages long, often internally contradictory and essentially consist of well-meaning but mostly misguided advice on how to improve the script. Frequently a new writer is brought in to do what is known as a polish. Many new writers can be brought in. Revisions can drag on for years. The film on the screen may bear very little resemblance to the original script.

Of all the credits on a film, the writing credit is always the most suspect. Often the person or persons credited on screen might not have written a single word of dialogue or a single scene that appears. Writers have become famous, have won awards, because of acclaimed films they didn't write. The Writers Guild arbitrates on contentious issues and almost always favours giving screen credit to the original writer even if he/she actually made only a minor contribution to the completed film.

In order to avoid the horrors of development hell an alternative these days is to go the independent route, which has led to independent films dominating the Academy Awards. Independent financing, for the director, means more creative control and much more flexibility over subject matter—the big studios now tend to favour remakes, action movies and adaptations of comic strips.

Independent film financiers are fairly new on the scene and fall into two groups: people who've made huge amounts of money in other fields, say, real estate, car franchises or arms dealing, and are besotted by the glamour of the movie business; or else they are governments of countries or states which are offering tax incentives or rebates to lure the film-makers to their locales.

Driving Miss Daisy was originally going to be financed by MGM, who then decided, even though the production contract was signed, that a movie about an old Jewish lady and her black chauffeur was not likely to bring in the punters. Disney toyed with the project for a while but Richard and Lili Zanuck and I refused to give in to their script and casting demands. They wanted a scene where the old lady and the chauffeur went nightclubbing together (in Atlanta in the 1940s!) and they thought Eddie Murphy was the ideal casting for the chauffeur, though he was far too young for the role. A lack of star names was one of our problems. But Richard, Lili and I were convinced that no one could play the roles better than Morgan Freeman and Jessica Tandy. So the search for finance continued.

The script went out to all of the Hollywood studios not previously approached, as well as possible financial sources in Europe. It was rejected all over the world. After a year or so of this we were about to give up, when Lili heard about a Canadian named Jake Eberts who had financed films in Europe, including *Chariots of Fire* and *The Name of the Rose* (1986). He was at a ski resort somewhere in Quebec. She sent him the script and he called us from the top of a mountain and said he'd put up $5 million of the $7.25 million budget.

For the remaining $2.25 million I called my old Australian friend Greg Coote, who had put some finance into *Breaker Morant.* He was now producing in Los Angeles. On the phone he told me he would definitely provide the funds we needed. I said I would send him the script. He protested that this was not necessary as he had faith in my judgment. I still insisted and the script was sent. The next day a call came from Greg: 'I will put this amount of money into any film you want to make,' he said, 'except this one.' The charm of Alfred Uhry's script escaped him, as it had so many others. He saw a film with an old black man and an old Jewish lady chatting in a kitchen as a commercial disaster. Hardly a controversial view, I had to admit, as I had doubts about its appeal myself, though I had nothing but admiration for Uhry's writing, his powers of observation, his humanity.

Richard Zanuck, a hugely successful ex-studio head himself, then persuaded Warner Bros. to invest the balance. They bowed to pressure and agreed—provided Richard and I deferred our modest producer and director fees. I cancelled my trip home to Australia and went off to Atlanta to look for locations. Ultimately, Jessica Tandy won the Academy Award for Best Actress and Alfred Uhry won Best Screenplay.

By the standards of most independently financed films

Driving Miss Daisy was uncomplicated. A few years later I spent an absurd amount of time, in association with a Los Angeles-based producer, trying to set up a film about the trumpeter Chet Baker. The first problem, a major one, was that our chosen actor, Josh Hartnett, was happy to have numerous meetings about the project, in which he bored me to tears with his endorsement of himself as a serious artist, but never went so far as to commit to the film.

I was asked if we could shoot the Californian scenes in Australia so advantage could be taken of a tax-incentive scheme. This, I agreed, was possible. Next, I was told of possible Canadian investment, so we would have to shoot the Paris scenes in Quebec. Also possible. Then it transpired that some Japanese investors weren't in favour of Josh Hartnett in the lead—not that he'd agreed to do it, in any case—and they also rejected all of the alternative names we proposed.

Financiers have a process they call running the numbers. With actor A, projected returns show that the film won't be worth investing in at, say, a budget of $15 million. Make it for $12 million and they'll consider it. Often it's impossible to cut the budgets, so the problem becomes that of persuading big-fee actors to work for, say, less than half of what they would normally receive. Not surprisingly, they usually stick to the huge fees and the studio-backed films.

European Union countries have become a key player in recent years. I'm sure everyone has seen those titles that say 'A British, French, Portuguese, Polish and Italian co-production.' These are known as 'Europudding' films. Many of them are surprisingly good: surprising, in view of the strange mixture of accents and talents involved. Negotiating with all the groups involved in setting up a Europudding film necessitates a producer with the organisational skill of Napoleon, the resilience of Ghandi and the guile of Atatürk. More and more films are being made in Europe in English and there are all sorts of tax incentives, as well as the lure of filming very cheaply in the former Iron Curtain countries.

I made a rather dismal film, *The Contract* (2006), almost entirely in Bulgaria, although it's set in America. We did two days' filming in the United States, mostly wide shots of towns, just to add a touch of credibility. I drew the line at casting actors speaking in Bulgarian with the idea of revoicing them later in English. I baulked at the idea of asking the leads, Morgan Freeman and John Cusack, to play their scenes without knowing what the other actors were saying. So we brought a supporting cast from London. The film was financed by an Israeli company based in Los Angeles—and they must've found their finance from a multitude of sources, as there are fourteen producers credited on the front titles. The writers credited were names unknown to me. They may have written a script entitled *The Contract*, but it was not the one I filmed.

I don't think that filmmaking was ever a pushover, though, and I believe that more often than not directors who have something to say will overcome the obstacles and make their films. There are a lot of committed and talented people around and a lot of very good movies still being made. Film is a great art form and I find it's even a lot of fun, along with a fair amount of frustration, dealing with all the problems.

2009

The Hubert Opperman Saga

Perhaps the oddest of the films that never happened—in my career so far—is the one involving Hubert Opperman.

Around 1990 a man named Clayton Sinclair, quite young and personable, approached me saying he had a screenplay about the Australian cyclist. Opperman (who died in 1996 at the age of ninety-one) was celebrated for his participation in the Tour de France in 1928 and 1930. In 1931 he won the Paris–Brest–Paris race of 726 miles—at that time the longest bicycle race in the world. Back in Australia he won numerous prizes, his crowning achievement being the 1940 Fremantle–Sydney race—2,875 miles on roads often so primitive that the bicycles had to be carried for miles over sand. Opperman's time of thirteen days knocked five days off the previous record. He joined the Liberal Party and had a distinguished political career, being at one time minister for shipping and transport; then, from 1963 to 1966, minister for immigration. He was knighted in 1968.

The script, by Peter Yeldham, was rather old-fashioned but capably told an exciting story of a young cyclist battling against poverty and official indifference to become one of the cycling greats.

Clayton, invariably cheerful and enthusiastic, told me that he and his business partner had been to a couple of Tour de France events with a film crew and shot footage of the races. I didn't see much point in this, as the Opperman races were fifty years previously and there was plenty of film material available of the modern ones. Clayton told me I could view the material he'd filmed but this was never arranged. I didn't pursue the matter, as I didn't think it could be substantially different from the various documentaries I'd already seen.

He came to London some months after our first meeting and asked me to give the script to any producers I knew. I assumed the point of this was to raise part of the finance for the film, as I was aware the budget would be well beyond that of virtually all Australian productions. I gave it to Guy East, a distinguished producer who had been associated with *Chariots of Fire*, among many other films.

Guy was enthusiastic and quickly offered to finance or part-finance the production. When I told Clayton this he responded by calmly telling me he didn't need any money as the film was *already* fully financed—at $26 million. When I asked why, in that case, we had bothered Guy East, he replied that he simply wanted to see if his original judgment of the value of the project was echoed by a reputable European producer.

I thought this was odd but wrote it off to the probability that Clayton was nervous about the project and the sizable budget. I had an embarrassing meeting with Guy at which I tried to explain the situation.

Back in Australia I assumed pre-production would begin almost immediately. With the finance in place I saw no reason not to begin casting and finding a crew. Clayton had mentioned approaching Mel Gibson to play Opperman but was vague about actually submitting the script to him, as he also was about engaging technicians, though he never ceased promoting the production in the press.

Becoming a little suspicious, I arranged for Clayton to meet the producer Sue Milliken, who was less gullible than me and had experience with a wide range of films. Clayton reiterated his assurance that the money to make the film was already in place and that soon everything would begin.

Sue and I discussed the matter at length. We tended to give Clayton the benefit of the doubt—what would be the point of making up the whole finance story? What could be gained, especially as an offer of finance from a successful producer in England had been turned down? The script existed and Peter Yeldham told us he had been paid a writing fee. In addition, there had been the trips to France to film a couple of the races. This wouldn't have been cheap, so there was finance from somewhere, though a disturbing newspaper item around this time reported that a travel agent was suing Clayton and his business partner over unpaid first-class tickets to France.

With some hesitation I arranged to meet the aged Hubert Opperman for lunch. I tentatively suggested to him that it was possible Clayton Sinclair was more interested in talking about the film than actually making it, as a few years had gone by without any progress.

Opperman, a courteous gentleman of the old school, replied that he had total faith in Clayton and had no doubt that all would be well. On a visit to Brisbane some time later I was contacted by Opperman's son, who told me that he, along with other family members, didn't trust Clayton and believed the film was a fantasy—of both his father and Clayton Sinclair.

Now desperate, but still convinced that the Opperman story could make a wonderful film, I contacted Peter Yeldham in the hope that the rights on the script might revert to him after a set period of time. If this was the case, Sue Milliken and I could take over the option and try to raise finance ourselves. No luck. The contract gave Clayton the rights in perpetuity.

I read in the *Sydney Morning Herald* that a group called the Australian Small Businessmen's Association could check on the bona fides of companies. I phoned the office number listed and explained the situation vis-a-vis Clayton Sinclair and the curiously stalled Opperman film. About a week later I had a cheerful phone call assuring me that Clayton's company expected a profit of $40 million in the forthcoming year.

Greatly relieved by this news, I asked its source, assuming that the Small Businessmen's Association would operate like MI5, skilfully ferreting out concealed information. I was stunned to be told that the source was Clayton himself. I protested that this was the equivalent of asking a murder suspect if he had committed the crime, then calmly accepting his denial as proof of innocence. The representative on the other end of the line was outraged by my attitude and demanded to know what I'd expected. 'Who did you think we could go to for information?' he asked, curtly.

One morning Clayton visited me at my house in Paddington. He was even more cheerful than usual and announced that this was a big day for him as a television series he was producing was commencing filming in Melbourne. Reassured by this information—for it gave Clayton credibility as a producer—I asked what the series was. A drama? Comedy? Who were the lead actors?

Immediately Clayton's attitude made a dramatic shift. He became angry and hostile, demanding to know why I wanted this information. Why, he asked, should he tell me anything about the television series? Why did I want to know? Taken aback, I said that there could hardly be any secret if cast and crew were already at work. And why couldn't I be trusted with the information, in any case? Who would I tell? And why? And what if I did? Television series usually thrive on publicity.

Once Clayton left I phoned my Los Angeles agent, Lenny Hirshan, and told him of the recent events. I mentioned that Clayton had repeatedly assured me that the $26 million for the film was already in the bank. Lenny said to tell him I had an old Jewish agent in America who never believed anybody and would he please send a bank statement by fax with details of the account. I phoned Clayton with this request. Cheerful once again, he said he would fax the information immediately. No fax ever arrived.

As far as I was concerned the whole business was finished. I am sure most directors would have abandoned ship much earlier, but I suppose I convinced myself that the whole affair was too elaborate to be a sham. What was there to be gained if there was no film and no possibility of one? Why spend all this time on the project? Why issue numerous press releases? Why travel to England and France? Why insist on the reality of non-existent finance? And so on.

Over the next few years I read occasional newspaper articles about the Opperman film going ahead—being produced by Clayton Sinclair. A phone call came one day from Nadia Tass, an accomplished Australian director who lives in Melbourne. She said she had heard I had been associated with the Opperman film and was curious about the experience. Clearly puzzled, she said she had been working on the project for some time with Clayton, but couldn't seem to actually prod him to begin practical production.

I heard no more about the television series that had aroused Clayton's ire. IMDb, which lists pretty well all film production worldwide, did not have his name listed.

Finally, at least ten years after our first meeting, I bumped into Clayton in the street in Balmain. He looked a little older but was as exuberant as ever. He told me a new script had been written about Opperman and his cycling career, and production on the film was about to commence.

2010

The Best Film I Never Made

I first read Boswell's *Life of Johnson* as a student at Sydney University. Needless to say, like most of the books I read, it wasn't on any of the courses that I was allegedly attending. It was not just the record of Johnson's wit that attracted me but the door that it opened onto another century: how they behaved, travelled, ate, thought, loved.

At this time, the early 1960s, a number of Boswell's diaries were being published after being found, with near-illegible handwriting and nibbled by rats, in various houses and even barns in Scotland. They were edited by an

American academic by the name of Frederick A. Pottle and dribbled onto the market at fairly long intervals with the addition of Pottle's (usually relevant) footnotes. Once again a window was opened onto life in the eighteenth century, the highlights, for me, being Boswell's descriptions of his trips around the Continent, his affair with an aristocratic Dutch girl, his meeting with Voltaire, and his numerous vividly described encounters with prostitutes followed by equally vivid descriptions of his efforts to cure his various sexual diseases, most of which seemed to include lemon juice and the insertion of hot glass rods into the male member.

It has always seemed a little odd to me that there have been no films about Johnson and Boswell, apart from a couple of BBC TV productions. The large, imperious and opinionated Englishman and the small drunken Scotsman were an ideal subject. Certainly, with Boswell's biography and all of the diaries, there is plenty of source material.

I was thrilled when a script arrived a few years ago, 'Boswell for the Defence', written by a Melbourne author, Patrick Edgeworth—a tall, courteous Englishman who emigrated to Australia as a young man and found work as a stand-up comedian, before becoming the author of a number of film scripts and quite a few plays. In his Boswell script Samuel Johnson makes no appearance at all, as the story deals with the later years of Boswell's life—when he was a down-and-out lawyer in London.

The days of celebrity that attended the publication of

the famous *Life* were over and Boswell was struggling to find work. A case was brought to his attention of a woman named Mary Broad, who had escaped from the penal colony in New South Wales (the only person ever to do so) and, after unbelievable hardships—which included the deaths of all her travelling companions and her children—had returned to London. She was arrested, imprisoned and threatened with execution as an escaped felon. Nobody wanted to defend her; nobody thought it worth their while; there would be no fee and little chance of success. This was not an era in which prisoners' rights were a factor.

Boswell took on the case and, amazingly, won it. Mary Broad was freed and went home to the west of England.

Patrick Edgeworth wrote a one-man stage play some years prior to the film script. This had huge success in the West End, with the Australian actor Leo McKern as Boswell.

The rewrite as a film script was so well thought-out, with added characters—including, of course, Mary Broad—integrated so seamlessly, that it was difficult to believe it was adapted from a one-man performance piece. I don't recall anything in any of the Boswell diaries about the trial, so either he never wrote anything or the indefatigable Frederick A. Pottle is still editing the text. (I just googled Pottle. He died in 1987.)

Patrick Edgeworth was able to get some information from contemporary newspapers, but the work is no doubt a largely brilliant invention based on his knowledge of Boswell from that chronicler's mountain of material written about himself. Devastatingly witty, the script is also compassionate and exciting as Boswell battles the indifferent lord chancellor (with whom he had studied law) for a reprieve for Mary Broad. Mary herself is cleverly realised—bitter and resentful as a result of her treatment, she at first finds it hard to believe that anyone in authority could be trying to help her.

I was so enthusiastic about the project that I swept aside my Hollywood agent's objections. He was dubious about the financial structure of the project, mainly because he was able to find out so little about it. He was also suspicious of European-based films made outside the studio system, cobbled together through a weird amalgam of sales agents, tax breaks and European film funds. If any one of various ninepins were to topple over the whole project could collapse.

The three producers involved also fitted into a pattern that caused concern. Nik Powell, the English partner, had been behind a number of films, some of them quite celebrated, but was renowned for his ability to skate on thin ice, with frequent falls. This didn't worry me unduly, as skating on thin ice is the modus operandi of most film producers, their projects being at the whim of capricious stars whose commitment could be withdrawn in the event of a better offer, or of studio executives whose ability to green-light could be suddenly extinguished by their fall from power. Rainer Mockert, the German fundraiser, was described to me as someone who 'sometimes comes through with the funding and sometimes doesn't'. The Australian producer, Mark Pennell, was a handsome ex-actor from *Neighbours*. Full of charm, he appeared to me to know virtually nothing about film production.

Pushing aside my agent's advice not to get involved I first headed off to San Diego, where I was restaging an opera production I had first directed in Houston—Carlyle Floyd's *Cold Sassy Tree*. I stopped off in Los Angeles to meet with Richard Dreyfuss who, I was told, was interested in playing Boswell. This struck me as an excellent idea. I'd worked with Richard before, in an unsuccessful film, *Silent Fall* (1994), and been impressed by his enormous talent (even if I tired of his tedious discussions of character motivation).

Richard knew nothing about Boswell, in fact didn't know the character wasn't fictional, but was most enthusiastic about the script. I thought that his quickness, humour and innate eccentricity made him perfect for the role. I knew, too, from seeing him play Fagin superbly in a Disney film of *Oliver Twist*, that accents were no problem to him.

While rehearsing *Cold Sassy Tree* with the great American soprano Patricia Racette in the leading role, I had a call from Nik Powell in London asking me to rush over, as pre-production meetings were necessary and it was not possible to wait for me until the end of the week. Reluctantly, I handed over the staging to my assistant, a likable ex-choirboy named Garnett Bruce, and flew off to London.

My suspicions that something was not shipshape with *Boswell* should have been aroused immediately when I was told, on arrival, that far from the production being brought forward, it was being pushed back some weeks. Why then did I have to hurry over from California? No answer was provided. A casual attitude was adopted by all, a ploy devised, no doubt, to allay anxiety (mine). Further, I was told that Richard Dreyfuss was no longer ideal for the leading role, as he was not considered a bankable star by distributors. Michael Caine had now been approached and was enthusiastic about the part.

There wasn't anything I could do. Caine was a popular actor, with an attractive manner on screen, though I don't think even he would claim to have the talent of Richard Dreyfuss. This business of films being, in effect, recast by investors and distributors had happened to me prior to this film and has happened a couple of times since. All my efforts at actually talking to the investors/distributors involved have been thwarted, leading me to think (though I've never been able to prove it) that the casting changes actually come about because of whims of the film's producers. Knowing that directors are likely to dig their heels in over certain casting choices and unwilling to confront them, they simply get out of the line of fire by inventing a distant and uncontactable villain.

I met with Nik Powell and Rainer Mockert, who hastened to assure me the delay had nothing to do with any financing problems, but was basically because of Michael Caine's availability. The meeting was in Nik's office, in Soho, a far cry from the elegant producers' offices I was familiar with in Los Angeles. It was up four flights of narrow stairs which needed careful negotiation because of the cardboard boxes piled haphazardly. The office itself was a shambles—a mess of papers and old posters. Nik himself was a lean, decrepit figure who would be rejected by Central Casting as a too-obvious rundown movie producer. He was friendly and talked very quickly, though it was curiously hard to catch his eye.

Rainer was more stylishly dressed (not a markedly difficult achievement), stocky and middle-aged, and spoke fluent English with a Second World War German officer accent. His main passion seemed to be opera and I began to suspect he was steering me onto this topic rather than discussing *Boswell*.

Once I had accepted the delay, pre-production went ahead. Michael Gambon, certainly one of the greatest actors working today, took the part of the lord chancellor and Samantha Morton the role of Mary Broad. I met Gambon backstage after he played in a revival of Pinter's *The Caretaker*, a play that seemed to me to be even better than

I remembered from the 1960s. He was affable and clearly yet another fan of Edgeworth's script. Samantha Morton, on the other hand, had a curiously hostile air, which I was told had something to do with her deprived background. Plenty of us have had to overcome that situation and it seems infantile to punish casual and guiltless acquaintances for it. However, I realised the hostility would work well in the role and Samantha's performance in Woody Allen's *Sweet and Lowdown* (1999) convinced me in one blow she was talented.

As production designer we engaged Martin Childs, a rather shy Englishman, who had long experience with the BBC and had won an Academy Award for *Shakespeare in Love* (1998). My regular first assistant director, the ebullient Rich Cowan, arrived from Vancouver. Probably the only forceful Canadian I've ever met, Rich is a brilliant organiser with an overwhelming passion for sports, including the arcane Canadian ones of curling and hockey. Peter James, the lighting cameraman (with whom I'd done *Driving Miss Daisy*, *Black Robe* and eight other films) arrived from Australia.

With reassurances from the producers that there were no hidden problems the aspect of film production I often find the most enjoyable began—location hunting. In a van, led by a glamorous young location manager from Yorkshire named Amanda Stevens ('I don't have affairs with married men'), we crashed around the south of England looking for grand country houses, eighteenth-century parks, eighteenth-century slums (Spitalfields was workable, despite being yuppified), coaching stations and so on.

During the long drives I taught everyone how to play the celebrity word game Botticelli. I remember winning a round with 'Joan Sutherland' and getting involved in a huge row with Rich Cowan, who insisted she couldn't lay claim to the title of celebrity, though he was quite happy to include various curling champions and regional Canadian hockey players in that category. To prove his point he leant out of the van at a traffic light and asked passers-by if they'd ever heard of someone named Joan Sutherland. No one had. I objected that this was hardly a fair test of celebrity. How many inhabitants of Slough would be familiar with the name of any opera star? I doubted if any of those asked would have heard of Julius Caesar or Genghis Khan either.

I think that mainly due to Amanda's attractiveness, allied with her straightforward manner—a characteristic of people from her part of England—we were granted filming access to one desirable location after another. In a visit to a grand country house owned by a cousin of the Queen we actually met the owner as we tramped around his lawns. Peter James was quick to inform him they were related. As taken aback as his good breeding would allow, the Queen's cousin said he was 'unaware of any relatives in Australia'. Rich Cowan and I were kicking Peter's ankles from opposite sides in an effort to quieten him, but he went on regardless with a tale of how his mother had assured him of the royal relationship. Peter was unconvinced of the absurdity of his claim even when I pointed out later that Australian mothers of that generation—his and mine—were nearly all anxious to claim exalted connections (the next generation was desperate to prove convict ancestry).

At Shepperton Studios a vast set of Newgate Prison, where Mary Broad was held, was under construction to Martin Childs' clever design. In the props department a number of sedan chairs were being built. They were the taxis of the late eighteenth century and would be needed for our numerous London street scenes. Costumes and props were being collected and filled huge storage rooms. The film seemed inevitable.

Suddenly, I was told that Samantha Morton would not be playing the lead female role. I could get no plausible explanation for this, although thought she might have become fed up with a number of mysterious changes to the start date. I talked to Nik Powell and Mark Pennell, asking them if Samantha had some information about the film that I didn't possess, such as, for example, that the finance was about to collapse? Absurd, I was assured, and told to get on with recasting the role.

Some weeks after Samantha's departure, with shooting only about nine days away, I was in the van with the crew when my mobile rang. Nik Powell was on the phone from Germany. The conversation was brief, just a few seconds—'There's no money. The film's off.' The mobiles (supplied by the production office) all stopped working a few minutes later. A day or so later the production office in Shepperton had gone. No one connected with the film could be found.

A few days later we held a morose 'end of no shoot' party in my London flat. None of the producers were present, just a depressed crew. The next day Rich Cowan and his wife returned to Vancouver, Martin Childs went onto the film *Quills* (2000), Amanda began location hunting for a new movie, and Peter James and I returned to Australia, at our own expense.

As I had a pay-or-play deal—if the film didn't go ahead I was supposed to collect my fee—I called my agent in Los Angeles. He phoned a few days later to say he couldn't find anyone connected with the production and the Byzantine contract led straight into a labyrinth, at the end of which was no fee for the director.

I have since often been asked why, if the script was so good, the cast in place and the film so close to production, finance couldn't be found to replace that which had presumably failed to materialise. I have no answer to the question, as I never found out anything at all about the structure, an obviously rickety one, behind the film. Perhaps too much money was owed? Had the huge set been paid for? Perhaps the German–English–Australian set-up was so complex no one could understand it, or perhaps the rights and percentage shares were already assigned in such a way there was no incentive left? It certainly seems to be the case that when films fall over at the last minute resuscitation is very rare.

A July 2014 check on the professional IMDb website revealed that Nik Powell continued to be associated with a number of films, though none of the titles were familiar to me. A decade earlier he had been appointed head of the National Film and Television School in Britain. Rainer Mockert had no credits since 2005, though a newspaper article some years later stated that he was producing *Doria*, to be directed by Dominic Minghella, and a Russian film, *Kolyma*. Neither of these films had yet been realised. Another article mentioned Rainer being associated with a number of opera productions. Mark Pennell was listed on IMDb as the producer of only one feature, *The Real Thing* in 2002, though an elaborate and laudatory biography stated that he had written and produced (in 2013) a $100-million feature film, *The Sea Hawk*, starring Hugh Jackman and directed by Martin Campbell. This film was not mentioned on the IMDb credits for either Jackman or Campbell. In 2014 there was no sign of its release.

...

Some months after returning to Sydney I received a call from Nik Powell's office to say the film was set up once again, and could I come to London to meet the new line producer, sign a production agreement and go on a location survey to Latvia (where it was cheaper to film than England)? I was hesitant, but my enthusiasm for the script was still so fervent that I brushed aside the warnings of my agent, lawyer, wife, family and friends.

In my London flat, Nik Powell was evasive but arranged for me to meet the line producer (whose name I can't recall), a bluff Englishman, clearly quite experienced. He, too, assured me the film would proceed, but the necessary papers couldn't be signed for a couple of weeks for some reason he didn't even attempt to explain. Naive to the last, I said I would go to Boston to visit my son, who had just joined the philosophy department at the University of Massachusetts.

When I returned to London I was told the papers were still not quite ready to be signed and there would be a delay of a few months. I knew this was the end of the line. I would never hear any more about the project. Defeated at last, I returned to Australia, realising I would never direct the brilliant screenplay Boswell for the Defence. *It will always be the best film I never made.*

2014

III

Behind the Screen

The Two Barrys

I've never been a great fan of comic strips. I'm probably missing out on something but only three ever held my attention for a long period. As a child I adored *Prince Valiant* and still remember the eponymous prince standing beside a huge pile of vanquished foes, his singing sword still in his hand. In those days, the 1950s, Hal Foster's superbly drawn strip was printed in one of the Sunday papers in colour.

I love Gary Trudeau's *Doonesbury* for the author's disenchantment with fashionably popular causes and ideas, and *Barry McKenzie* because of Barry Humphries' unpredictably pointed satire, humour, and ear for the vagaries and vulgarities of Australian English.

I first met Barry McKenzie and Barry Humphries around the same time and in the same place—London, the mid-1960s. I had returned to England anxious to avoid the looming Biafran War, in which a number of my Nigerian friends were subsequently killed, and was intent on somehow sliding past the obstructive film union and finding work in the film business.

The *Barry McKenzie* strip (at that time, amazingly, banned in Australia) was running in the satirical magazine *Private Eye*, where McKenzie's outrageous adventures among the Poms and, in particular, his scatological remarks and euphemisms for bodily discharges and fornication were a source of discussion and wonder. I noticed that Barry Humphries was performing with Spike Milligan in a Christmas production of *Treasure Island* at the Mermaid Theatre. Both actors improvised wildly, to such effect that the play, scheduled to close in mid-January, ran until April.

Armed with a casual suggestion from Patrick White to 'give Barry a call' I marched backstage, rather warily, after a performance and introduced myself. Expecting nothing more than a few pleasantries, I was surprised at Barry's amiability and what appeared to be a genuine interest in my pretty well non-existent career.

Now that I've been friends with Barry for over fifty years and have directed him in four feature films, I'm often asked if he (a) is difficult to work with, (b) is crazy, (c) is unreliable and (d) believes he is really Edna Everage. The answer to all four questions is no, though (c) could apply occasionally. He can certainly become Edna Everage when performing—in the way that all great actors can inhabit whoever it is they are impersonating—but the shift back to his own personality can be so striking that I have attended stage performances where I heard the people sitting around me loudly refusing to believe that the urbane man receiving applause could possibly be the woman they have been watching for an hour or more.

Barry has always struck me as good-humoured and even-tempered. His relations with his fellow actors, stage crews and film technicians is always cordial. I am jealous of his ability to remember everyone's name, even if he bumps into them some years after the time he was working with them on a stage show or film set. In contrast, I have sometimes met actors I have directed and been unable to remember not only their name but in which film of mine they appeared.

He has a wide range of interests. His reading is vast and is greatly aided by his irritating recall of detail. He seems to have read everything in his enormous and well-catalogued library—one that ranges from an unpublished short story by F. Scott Fitzgerald (in his own handwriting) to the arcane novels of Marmaduke Pickthall.

I find his collection of paintings even more fascinating.

There are few works, very few, by artists who are household names but many charmingly decorative works (quite a few of them of attractive ladies) by mainly European painters of the period 1880 to 1940, although there are also oils and sketches by American and Australian artists. It is the collection of a man with impeccable and individual taste, unimpressed by the fleetingly fashionable and guided only by a response to beauty. I have not heard him express admiration for Basquiat or Cy Twombly. Barry is a keen painter himself, and it has always fascinated me that his wild and colourful landscapes bear no affinity with the pictures that he collects.

It has puzzled me, especially over the past five years, to hear Barry occasionally referred to as right-wing. I'm not at all sure what this means these days. I was once called 'right-wing' when I told a leftist friend that I favoured a multi-party to a one-party political system. There was criticism recently when Sir Les Patterson, a politician and one of Barry's creations, spoke on behalf of the cartoonist Bill Leak, who had died, perhaps from stress, after being persecuted over the content of one of his cartoons. Sir Les spoke in favour of freedom of speech, a point of view that strikes me as admirable. It seems to be an odd concept to advocate boundaries on the subject matter of a political cartoonist.

I can remember few political comments from Barry apart from an admiration he once expressed for John

Howard, a sentiment that was shared by many fellow Australians, who re-elected him as prime minister three times. On another occasion, some years ago, Barry expressed fury over the fact that in the 1930s the Australian government restricted entry to the country to many of the Jews fleeing the insanity of Hitler.

Back to *Barry McKenzie*. It was some time in 1968 that I suggested to Barry Humphries that a feature film could be made from the comic strip. He doubted that the character could sustain a full-length movie but agreed that this would depend largely on finding someone who fitted the role perfectly. About a year later he called me from Sydney and expressed enthusiasm about a singer he had met named Barry Crocker who had a 'great big chin'—an essential attribute of the comic-strip version of McKenzie. I didn't think a chin was the sole qualification for the role, but was just as enthusiastic when I met Crocker in 1971. I've always admired the easy charm and innocence he brought to Bazza—it enabled us to get away with the most ribald euphemisms.

Initially, Barry gave me all of the old comic strips so that I could lift scenes, characters and dialogue for the film script. I even had some material that the artist, Nick Garland, considered in such poor taste that he refused to illustrate it. There was also a fairly detailed outline of a McKenzie musical that Barry had written, and abandoned, some years previously. I can imagine the reaction of West

End managements when presented with the songs 'Don't Tread in the Poop on the Pavement' and 'The One-Eyed Trouser Snake'. I didn't show such refinement and included the second of these in the film, where it was sung by the unlikely combination of Barry Crocker and Julie Covington. Julie, now forgotten, had a superb voice and was the original Evita. She is on the first recording but mysteriously turned down an offer from Andrew Lloyd Webber to play the role on stage.

When Barry returned to London we spent some weeks together preparing the final version of the script. There was still no finance for the film, but with the help and enthusiasm of Phillip Adams the backing (around $250,000) was provided by the somewhat reluctant Australian Film Commission. 'Delete all the Australian slang from the script,' was their final directive just before production started—advice which, if followed, would have resulted in a film only a few minutes long.

I once asked Barry how much of Barry McKenzie's vocabulary was invented and how much was real. Virtually all of it was real, he said, and I realised, as I listened more carefully to how Australians actually spoke, that Barry had the acuteness to pinpoint phrases from ordinary conversations that would normally pass unnoticed. I know that he eavesdropped on people in bars and restaurants and, of course, he forgot nothing. After much insistent questioning, however, he admitted that one phrase was entirely his invention. Interestingly, it is perhaps the most famous of all of McKenzie's bon mots: 'point Percy at the porcelain'.

When *Private Eye* dropped *Barry McKenzie* the comic strip was at the peak of its popularity. The reasons given were, variously, that Barry missed some delivery dates for the material (probably true) and also that the ex-public-school boys publishing the magazine had forged social links with the royal family, so had become wary of printing too much of McKenzie's humour at their expense, especially after one celebrated episode where McKenzie found himself inside Buckingham Palace, where he disturbed the Queen on the lavatory.

The Adventures of Barry McKenzie was commercially successful in Australia but horrific reviews focused on its vulgarity being bad for the country's image. Barry Humphries and I were both taken aback at the vitriol, which was unexpected. Perhaps naively, we had imagined it was all just harmless fun. The censorship board gave the film an X rating, which forbade almost any audience from attending, but after we pointed out there was no nudity in the film, no sex (McKenzie always shied away from it) and no bad language but just a lot of euphemisms, the rating was revised to a G, which meant anyone at all could attend a screening.

A sequel, *Barry McKenzie Holds His Own* (1974), was less successful but, I thought, even funnier than the first one. Again, the critics were hostile in the extreme and I could see my career as a film director coming to a halt. Ostracised locally, I went back to England and directed a lamentable rock musical. While contemplating opening a second-hand bookshop I had a phone call from Phillip Adams asking if I would be interested in making a film of *Don's Party*. I am sure other directors had been approached before me but had baulked at the prospect of directing eleven actors in one small house for the entire action of the film. I think I was too ignorant to be aware of the problems, and was an admirer of David Williamson's writing, so happily took on the task and gained some critical credibility.

The two McKenzie films seem to be regarded now with an affection denied them at the time of their release.

Barry Crocker, a most likable man, is still living in Sydney. He was forty-two when the first McKenzie film was made but played a twenty-four-year-old with ease.

Barry Humphries, now in his eighties, is still performing all over the world. Last year, while he was doing his one-man stage show in Los Angeles, I had a call from him to see if I would like to pick him up and drive with him to Pasadena, where he had heard there was a formidable second-hand bookshop. Halfway to Pasadena, on the freeway, his phone rang. It was the stage manager of Barry's show at the Ahmanson Theatre, enquiring as to his whereabouts as the theatre was full for the matinee.

Barry had forgotten all about the matinee. I turned the car around on the freeway and headed back to Los Angeles, assuring him as I did so that the audience would have to wait, as the show couldn't begin without him. I dropped him at the stage door a few minutes before the curtain was due to go up. I found out later that he managed to appear on stage, made up as Edna Everage, on time.

Virginia, my wife, and I went to the show again on the final night. The theatre was full. It was full every night of the six-week run. It could have continued for months but Barry had another commitment in London.

2008; 2017

Memories of Horton Foote

In 1980 my feature film *Breaker Morant* attracted some notice outside Australia, mainly because it was selected for competition in Cannes. For the first time agents who had long shown a strong lack of interest in my career began to call and scripts began to arrive at my house in Sydney from the United States. I remember stacking them vertically in a pile by a chair in the living room, sitting down with an air of importance and beginning to read.

Not surprisingly, most were indifferent. Many were formulaic comedies or melodramas, often written by people who had only a passing acquaintance with English grammar. After a couple of days, around two-thirds of the way down the stack, I picked up a script entitled 'Tender Mercies'. This gentle story of a down-and-out country-and-western singer and his relationship with a Vietnam war widow and her young son captivated me from the first page. The dialogue I found particularly impressive. It was simple, straightforward; it never seemed to strive for effect and was devoid of the one-line gags so characteristic of film scriptwriters. I found it almost unbearably moving and was quite sure it was written with a precise ear for the cadences and phrases of the Texans among whom the story was set.

Immediately thinking that the script could be with other directors and without even getting to the end of the story I phoned the producers in New York, Philip and Mary-Ann Hobel, and told them I would direct the film. A trip to Texas was arranged so that I could see the location, an attractive town called Waxahachie—and meet the writer, Horton Foote. This was to be only my second visit to the United States. Previously I had visited a film-critic friend in New York—a charming man who came to a ghastly end when a gay lover smashed his head in with a frying pan.

In those pre-internet days it wasn't so easy to find information on people. Although I knew that Horton had won an Academy Award for his adaptation of *To Kill a Mockingbird*, I had no idea that he was a celebrated playwright. (It still strikes me as odd that even today none of his plays have been performed in Australia.)

Over the next twenty-five years I saw productions of a number of his plays and read others. I rank him, for what my opinion is worth, among the finest of twentieth-century writers. Critics who say that he writes within the narrow range of the people he knows, a statement presumably meant as a criticism, are making no point at all. All of the greatest writers, from Tolstoy to Dickens to Chekhov and Tennessee Williams, have done this. That Horton wrote wisely and inexhaustibly about the characters and events in a small Texas town is to his credit, not his detriment.

Horton must have been around sixty-five when we first met. Even in the Texas heat he always wore what seemed to be a heavy woollen jacket, plus a tie. He was handsome, with a thick thatch of snowy white hair. I always hoped that at the same age my hair would be as thick—the colour didn't worry me. Unfortunately, my mother's family genes won the battle.

His manner was gentle and his face appropriately kindly in demeanour. He was one of those rare people, perhaps the only one I've met, who looked on the world with goodwill and saw the best aspects of everyone. In return, his benign qualities were instinctively recognised by everyone with whom he came in contact and they behaved accordingly. The toughest Texans did not raise their voices or use bad language in his presence; the most frustrated and irascible waiters and shop assistants were courteous in their dealings with him.

His eyes were large and can only be described as beautiful. They glowed with, it seemed to me, the kindness and sweetness of his nature, but also with intelligence and perspicacity. When I saw him just a few months before his death in 2009 his body was feeble, but his acuteness was undiminished and his eyes as clear and brilliant as always.

Horton is one of the few people I have met who could be both entertaining and interesting without ever making derogatory comments or criticisms of his many past collaborators—writers, directors or actors. Again, he saw only the best of what they had to offer. Quite an achievement, considering some of the notoriously self-centred and self-promoting people with whom he had to deal.

Working with him on *Tender Mercies* remains a high point of my directing experiences. An outstanding cast did a wonderful job, aided immeasurably by Horton's superb dialogue. I know, from my other films, that the most gifted actors can do little if the language is pedestrian.

I was thrilled when, a few days before I began writing this piece, my twenty-three-year-old daughter, studying at a film school in California, called me to say she'd just seen *Tender Mercies* and considers it one of her favourite films. It is one of mine, just as Horton Foote is one of my very favourite people.

2009

John Simon on Film: An Introduction

Like most film directors I have a detestation of movie critics, based, of course, on their failure to recognise the amazing talent displayed in all of my works, while they all too often praise the feeble efforts of my contemporaries. Though I've never gone so far as a celebrated Australian playwright friend of mine, who sought out his detractors and physically assaulted them. I have, with effort, followed the advice of Raymond Chandler and never responded to criticism.

The numerous readers of the film criticism of John

Simon will no doubt attribute this piece to his favourable reviews of my films *Tender Mercies*, *Driving Miss Daisy*, *Mister Johnson* (1990) and *Black Robe*. He is even moderately kind about *A Good Man in Africa* (1994), which I considered disastrous. His reviews of *Paradise Road* and *Bride of the Wind*, both of which I still irrationally maintain were not all that bad, are dismissive if annoyingly acute.

I met John for the first time in 1977 at the Berlin Film Festival. I was there with an Australian film, *Don's Party*, which was written by my two-fisted playwright friend, David Williamson. After the screening I went to one of those desultory drinks parties where lots of people circle one another warily, not being too sure of who is associated with the film and who isn't. John, displaying no caution, was at the centre of what seemed to me to be an awestruck crowd. I had no idea who he was. I had never been to America and knew virtually nothing of the New York critics. I eavesdropped for a while, amused by John's precise and witty opinions. Being young and hardy, I introduced myself as the director of *Don's Party*. John nodded for a few moments, then said it was 'not without merit'.

A couple of years later I was in New York, promoting *Breaker Morant*—my major appearance of behalf of that film was an interview on an all-nude (except for me) late-night talk show, which was being transmitted from a sleazy room in an even more sleazy building. John had given me his number and I tentatively called him, not expecting him to remember me.

He did remember, though, and we met for lunch. We quickly discovered a mutual interest in theatre, as well as film, and a passion for the more obscure classical composers. For years after, we jointly ransacked Tower Records in search of the works of Bantock, Montsalvatge, York Bowen, Hovhaness, Moeran, Guarnieri and others near forgotten but gifted.

By this time I'd read a lot of John's work, not just his film writing, but articles on theatre and music. He seemed to me to have more knowledge that it was possible to acquire in a lifetime, yet he was no pedant. He has a vast range of interests, speaks five or six languages fluently, and responds with vigour to everything that crosses his path.

The point I am lurching towards is that I find John's critical writing immensely entertaining even when I'm not in agreement with him—and who could possibly agree with a critic's views on every film? Mostly, I find, I do agree. More importantly, I find his reviews full of insights and perceptions that makes reading a collection of his work as exciting as reading a gripping novel.

It is clear to me, too, that despite John's extraordinary erudition his response to each film under discussion is fundamentally an emotional one. He is moved by the power of cinema—by its stories, its characters, its themes. He then has the gift, such a rare one (especially among film critics), of being able to analyse the work in question, to be able to say why it is that it's so powerful, so touching; or, on the other hand, so trite, so meretricious or so banal. He is, perhaps, rather inclined to be more forgiving of the weaknesses of beautiful young actresses than he is of actors, writers or directors, but this is a factor I find perfectly understandable. I know it isn't politically correct to say it, but…watching beautiful girls can do a lot to relieve tedium.

John's wit is dazzling and is never displayed for its own sake, but to drive home an aspect of the review. Writing about Bergman's *Fanny and Alexander* (1982) he says: 'it is all dismally attitudinising and hollow, a sort of cross between Carl Dreyer at his worst and John Fowles at his best, which is not far removed from his worst.' I feel he's being a bit tough on *Fanny and Alexander*, though it is somewhat sententious, but he couldn't be more on the money with the comment on Fowles. Reviewing Candice Bergen's performance in *Gandhi* (1982), he writes, 'though she is a bit of a real-life photographer, Miss Bergen does not even handle a camera convincingly, albeit this is nothing compared to what she does with acting.'

It takes courage (sheer foolhardiness, in my case) to speak out against widely held views relating to current films. One tends to end up being categorised with the man who said Beethoven was a lousy composer or that Tolstoy couldn't write. I recall being ostracised at dinner parties for my perhaps not-too-timidly expressed reservations about *The Piano* (1993) and *The English Patient* (1996). It thrills me to read the abandon with which John Simon tears into the sacred cows of cinema: 'how long has it been since an

American movie has garnered a harvest of laurels like the one being heaped on a piece of mindless junk called *Blue Velvet*.' On Kurosawa's *Ran* (1985): 'I find it an almost total failure by a genius in his old age.'

His comment on Fellini must have outraged most of that director's vast following, but I feel that time will prove it to be correct: 'when he made his early, wonderful movies, Fellini was a natural talent—perhaps the most natural of all. Despite a distinctly autobiographical flavour, the films managed to be sufficiently different.' He considers the best of them to be *I Vitelloni* (1953) and thinks *8½* (1963) to be Fellini's 'last film to show intermittent strength'. What went wrong? 'Success and egomania, and detachment from the world; withdrawal behind a living wall of amateur adulators and professional sycophants.'

Writing about Agnieszka Holland's *Europa Europa* (1990): 'the fact that it takes on an important subject seems to have guaranteed it good notices from the more Pavlovian reviewers.' Simon examines, with characteristic logic, the many inconsistencies in the plot, finishing with the telling remark, 'what good is all the truth in the world if the work of art cannot make it feel true?'

It's been said to me, of John Simon's reviews in general, that he is merely iconoclastic, that virtually nothing has his approbation. The comment seems a bizarre one, as even the most cursory examination of his reviews will reveal enthusiasm for a huge number of films.

It is much easier to write scathing reviews than adulatory ones, but Simon expresses praise as fluently and entertainingly as his dislikes. He begins a review of Bille August's wonderful *Pelle the Conqueror* (1987): 'it won the Golden Palm in Cannes and the Oscar for best foreign film of 1988. The remarkable thing is that, despite these awards, it is a very good film.' Nor does he ignore or automatically dismiss mainstream cinema, even if he consistently shows a preference for the undoubtedly more personal products of the independents. He quickly dismisses both *Gladiator* (2000) and *Titanic* (1997) but finds Scorsese's *Goodfellas* (1990) 'the most original and assured piece of American mainline cinema since—it's been so long. I've forgotten what.' He considers Jim Sheridan's *In the Name of the Father* (1993) 'a great film…it is something with which to bolster audiences: fill 'em up with pity and terror, with laughter, sadness, and rage. And perhaps even—the hardest reaction to elicit from moviegoers—thought.'

It was exciting for me to read through his writings and see such warm praise for so many films that I feel have been unjustly ignored, or which have had only limited screenings—Zhang Yimou's *Not One Less* (1999), Gillies MacKinnon's *Regeneration* (1997), Cédric Klapisch's *When the Cat's Away* (1996), Robert Benton's *Nobody's Fool* (1994), Pavel Chukhrai's *The Thief* (1997), James Ivory's *Mr. and Mrs. Bridge* (1990), Francesco Rosi's *The Truce* (1997). There are many others. Now, with the ubiquity of DVD and online streaming, readers can see nearly all of the films John Simon enthuses about. They are not going to be disappointed.

It is refreshing, too, to read a reviewer who is aware of the contributions made to a film by people other than the director and actors. These reviews often mention and discuss the work of cameramen, set designers, editors, costume designers and composers. The last, whose contribution has assumed greater prominence in films because of developments in sound reproduction, come in for a broadside more often than not: 'hack composers provide rampaging scores that tautologically hammer in obvious points—or, worse yet, blurt out that big moments are ahead.' Cameramen fare much better. Writing about *Faithless* (2000), a superb film written by Ingmar Bergman and directed by Liv Ullmann, Simon says: 'one of the film's remarkable features is the preponderance of scenes tightly confined within four walls, yet such is Persson's artistry with light and shadow and shades of colour that his cinematography contributes as much emotion as some filmmakers' entire movies.'

How do we know if it's a great film? I think John Simon's recommended test is infallible. In an aside from a review of Erick Zonca's brilliant *The Dreamlife of Angels* (1998) he notes: 'the surest way of testing a movie's greatness is seeing it a second time. If it is just as good, it is a good film. If it gets better in the fineness and fullness of its detail, it is great.'

2005

Dino De Laurentiis, Producer

I first met Dino De Laurentiis sometime in 1985. I knew his name from the credits of a staggering number of Italian films, the first of which he'd produced in 1940. As a student I had frequently made the journey into central Sydney and its (then) one art house, the Paris, where Dino's name was prominently displayed on the titles of the kind of movies that made me want to become a director: *Bitter Rice* (1948), *La Strada* (1954), *The Nights of Cabiria* (1957). Associated with Carlo Ponti, he became the pioneer of Italian-American epics of the *War and Peace* (1956, directed by King Vidor) variety.

In 1985, having directed a few films in America (beginning with *Tender Mercies*), I saw Beth Henley's play *Crimes of the Heart* on Broadway and was determined to make it into a movie. Despite initial enthusiasm from various studios, apathy soon set in as the usual anonymous readers' reports—written by the scantily educated and deeply insensitive, a notably formidable combination—branded the script as negligible, though it was adapted by Henley and the play had won the 1981 Pulitzer Prize.

Undaunted, or only slightly daunted, I discussed the matter with the producer, Freddie Fields, who suggested we take the project along to Dino De Laurentiis. By this time, Dino had given up on his Italian-American epics, because of a row with the Italian tax authorities it was rumoured, and moved his entire operation, at an age when many men are thinking of retiring, to Los Angeles. He'd already confounded cynics—convinced he'd never be able to function out of Italy—with films as diverse as *The Shootist* (1976), *Flash Gordon* (1980), *Ragtime* (1981) and *Conan the Destroyer* (1984).

I was wary about approaching him with a story about three sisters in the Deep South, one which relied to a large extent on the writer's acute observation of Mississippi speech patterns—something I was certain would be lost on Dino, who, I was told, spoke only a smattering of English and an incomprehensible smattering at that.

I feared the worst at our first meeting when I was

ushered into a vast office somewhere on Wilshire Boulevard and saw a small man with penetrating eyes and a determined jaw behind a huge desk. He left the desk immediately, greeted me warmly, signalled to someone to bring espresso and launched, with no small talk, into an enthusiastic analysis of *Crimes of the Heart.* His command of English was certainly terrible but it hardly mattered, as his dynamism made his points perfectly clear. Although he'd only had the script a couple of days he'd had it translated into Italian and seemed to have a total grasp of its characters and situations, as well as an ability to recall the most minute details.

Over the years that I knew Dino perhaps the aspect of him that most impressed is that he actually read all the scripts submitted (surprisingly rare among producers) and was able to analyse their strengths and weaknesses remarkably succinctly and, in my opinion, accurately. He relied on his instincts—another plus in my book, as films should be made because of passion not an analysis of market trends. He frequently bewildered his colleagues with snap judgments, often involving huge expenditure and the hiring or non-hiring of major actors and directors.

Some months after *Crimes of the Heart* was completed Dino asked me to come into his office, as he had a few questions about Australia. With no preamble, he threw a fairly basic map of the continent onto the desk and asked me where films were made. I pointed to Sydney and Melbourne. He then asked where people go for their holidays. With a slight hesitation I indicated the Gold Coast—an area of splendid beaches and horrible urban development. Australia's Miami.

'That's it!' Dino informed the various people dotted around the room. 'That's where we build a film studio.' A few people looked slightly startled, but most of them, no doubt familiar with Dino's abrupt decisions, just nodded. 'But,' I said, 'there are no facilities up there. No technicians live there. There are no actors. You'd have to import everyone.' 'No problem,' Dino rejoined, in fractured English I can't hope to reproduce here. 'You said it's a holiday place. Then they all like to go there!' This seemed an unlikely proposition to me. Hundreds of people would have to relocate their lives away from major cities to a relatively remote part of the country.

I left the room and called some producer friends in Australia, all of whom echoed my feeling that a studio on the Gold Coast would be a fiasco. Dino went ahead all the same, with Byzantine financial arrangements that I think only he understood. And he was proved right: the Gold Coast studios have been operating successfully for over twenty years. Technicians did happily relocate and producers from all over the world make numerous films and television shows there.

Dino was no intellectual in the conventional sense. I cannot imagine him spending much (any?) time reading novels or poetry (unless there was a possible film involved) and I never heard him talk about painting or music. He was devoted to his family, loved watching football on television and was a first-class cook, especially of Neapolitan dishes. When we were in Rome together and went to restaurants he always insisted on inspecting the kitchens before placing an order. We were invariably taken on a guided tour by the obsequious restaurant owner, who would watch anxiously as Dino prodded the meat and checked the fish and vegetables for freshness.

Dino had innate good taste and was as shrewd a judge of directors, designers, cameramen, composers and actors as he was of scripts. He insisted I use an Italian cameraman, Dante Spinotti, on *Crimes of the Heart*, as he'd seen a low-budget sword-and-sandal epic Dante had photographed and thought he had immense talent. He was right. Spinotti came to America and went on from *Crimes* to such remarkable-looking films as *Last of the Mohicans* (1992) and *The Insider* (1999).

I am not implying that Dino is infallible. Far from it. Rather, he had the ability shared by all really successful producers (and directors) to be able to bounce back from failure and move on to the next project. I remember the opening of *Tai-Pan* (1986, directed by Daryl Duke), an adventure film with Bryan Brown that was slaughtered by the critics and ignored by the public. Dino spent a disconsolate morning after the premiere and everyone moved around the office as if a loved one had just died. I hated seeing Dino glum and didn't know what to say. But after lunch the fire was back in his eyes and he enthused to me, in fractured but forceful English, about a new project he had that was going to be wonderful.

As a producer on *Crimes of the Heart* he was attentive and encouraging. He rolled up to the rushes every night in a vast car, greeted everyone from the stars to the grips with equal courtesy and watched the previous day's work. Like Richard Zanuck and Placido Domingo (and perhaps no one else with whom I've worked) he had the knack of spreading goodwill, a feeling of unity, that brought out the best in everyone: actors and crew alike.

He seemed to be free of malice or bitterness. I can't actually recall him saying anything nasty about anyone, with the exception of a few lawyers and employees of the Internal Revenue Service—largely, I suppose, because he was more concerned about the future than the past. I've been told, though, that he was quite capable of instinctive dislikes. One acclaimed antipodean director, I heard, was collected at the airport by Dino, who decided straight away that he didn't like him, then dumped him in a hotel for a night and returned him—no doubt mightily bewildered—to the Antipodes the next morning.

I'm pleased to say this treatment eluded me. I was the recipient of the friendship of a remarkable man. 'How did you produce your first film?' I asked him at one of his fabled dinner parties. 'I was seventeen,' he told me. 'I saw this Swedish film, in Italy. I thought it was a good story. I went into the cinema and watched it over and over again, writing down the dialogue in the dark. I then reworked it as a story set in Italy and persuaded someone to make it.' That was in 1939. Dino died in 2010, at the age of ninety-one, having produced one hundred and fifty feature films.

2011

Tony Scott, Director

On 19 August 2012, the film director Tony Scott parked his car on a bridge over Los Angeles harbour, climbed a twelve-foot wire fence and jumped to his death without hesitating. He had just completed shooting a new film and associates said that he appeared, a couple of days before the leap, to be as optimistic and buoyant as ever. There was a rumour that he had brain cancer (denied by his family) and also that he suffered bouts of depression.

In a staggeringly successful career Tony directed seventeen feature films (*Top Gun*, *Unstoppable* and so on), virtually all of them commercially successful. The various obituaries for Tony usually list his first feature as *The Hunger* in 1983—a film slaughtered at the time by critics, but admired now for Tony's visual flair and dynamic editing style. *The Hunger*, however, was not actually the first feature directed by Tony, although it was certainly the first to achieve wide distribution.

...

From 1965 to 1971 I ran the British Film Institute's Production Board, a small-scale filmmaking unit set up in London with the aim of helping young filmmakers get started in an industry which was shackled at that time by archaic union rules that prevented recruitment. There were numerous applicants for our modest budgets and facilities. It was my job to assess the feasibility of all the submitted projects, then present them to a committee of eminent arts figures.

I expected to have endless problems with a committee that appeared to me to be out of touch with the swinging sixties. This proved not to be the case. The youngest of them would have been at least double my age, but all were frighteningly well-informed and were quick to spot originality and talent in the mass of applicants, among them Tony Scott.

Tony was twenty-one in 1966 when he first came to the BFI production office, hidden away in the middle of a street market called Lower Marsh, behind Waterloo station. He was friendly, cheerful, even ebullient, and spoke with a Northern accent (an accent that filmed interviews shown after his death reveal he never lost). He screened a short film directed by his brother, Ridley, 'Boy and Bicycle'. Tony was the eponymous boy. I could see immediately that Ridley was vastly talented (his later successes include *The Duellists* in 1977, *Gladiator*, and *Black Hawk Down* in 2001).

But did this gift extend to his young brother? Tony wanted to make a short film from a story by Ambrose Bierce set in the American Civil War, 'One of the Missing'. I thought this an ambitious undertaking for a novice film-maker, but changed my mind rapidly when Tony produced a set of beautifully drawn storyboards detailing every shot through the entire thirty-minute film. Tony and Ridley were both students at the Royal College of Art and could both draw like Raphael—at least, that was the way it seemed to me (someone whose drawing skill has still not progressed past stick figures).

Tony edited the film in the Waterloo editing room, so we were in daily contact. He was hard-working, meticulous and always amiable. For relaxation he climbed mountains in Scotland and Wales, and he would terrify his friends by doing handstands on the edges of city buildings. He had no fear of heights, or of anything else, it seemed. On one occasion he was refuelling his car late at night when three large West Indians pulled up and began to make comments about a small man like Tony driving a smart sports car. They began to push him around and he retaliated by flattening all three. They responded by suing him for assault. In court, the judge took one look at the three men and then at the diminutive Tony and dismissed the case.

Despite some objections from the BFI board that Tony's style was 'commercial', rather than 'experimental'—vague appellations that all too often could be more accurately defined as 'professional' and 'amateurish', respectively—a budget was approved that enabled him to make a black-and-white feature film, *Loving Memory.* This sensitive film is the only one Tony Scott ever made that drew on his North Country background. It told of a brother and sister on a remote farm who accidentally kill a cyclist, then take the body back to the house, where the lonely sister keeps it in the attic, makes it cups of tea and engages in one-sided conversation. Macabre—but oddly delicate and touching. Well photographed by Chris Menges, it won the Opera Prima at the Venice Film Festival in 1971.

Apart from an occasional message from mutual industry friends, I lost touch with Tony after 1973. I know that everyone who worked with him loved him—for his dedication, his good humour, his straightforward North of England manner. A few actors complained that he was more interested in visuals than their performances, but actors always complain, as they believe any film is about nothing but them.

Why did Tony Scott jump from that bridge in Los Angeles? I doubt if we will ever know, though there are no doubt people who do know.

At the time Tony made his Civil War film, 'One of the Missing', he was inspired by a French film adapted from another Ambrose Bierce story, 'An Occurrence at Owl Creek Bridge'. He and I watched it a number of times. The story is about a prisoner of war who dies when he jumps from a bridge into the river below.

2012

Robert Krasker: A Sketch

The Australian cinematographer Robert Krasker died on 16 August (my birthday) in 1981.

Krasker had a remarkable career, entirely in Europe, and is unquestionably one of the greatest lighting camerapersons (impossible to say cameraman these days, as there are a number of notable women cinematographers) of all time. Regrettably, photographers of movies never achieve the worldwide recognition of still photographers such as Eugène Atget, Irving Penn, Henri Cartier-Bresson, Annie Leibovitz, Josef Sudek, Ansel Adams, Robert Capa and so many others, as their work doesn't appear in accessible book form or in exhibitions and their screen credits whizz through in small type after those of usually overpraised actors.

Born in 1913 in Egypt to Romanian parents who emigrated to Western Australia when he was a few months old, Krasker left Australia in 1930 and studied art for some months in Paris and photography in Dresden. He spoke fluent French and German. He went to England in 1932 and joined Alexander Korda's London Films as a camera assistant. He worked with the distinguished French lighting cameraman Georges Périnal (1897–1965) on the spectacular colour epics *The Four Feathers* (1939) and *The Thief of Bagdad* (1940).

His first film as lighting cameraman was *The Gentle Sex*, directed by Leslie Howard in 1943. But it was his association with the greatest of all the British directors, Carol Reed (1906–76), that marked him as a photographer of startling talent. His black-and-white photography was full of striking high-contrast images and bold wide-angle compositions. *Odd Man Out* (1947), Reed's stunning film with James Mason as an IRA man on the run in Belfast, is as impressive today as it was on its release. I would rank it among the ten greatest films of all time.

This was followed by *The Third Man* in 1949. This time it was Orson Welles' drug dealer Harry Lime on the run in Vienna. Krasker's atmospheric creation of the rundown post-war city is unforgettable, and quite remarkable considering that most of the film was shot on the sound stages of Korda's London studios. Robert Krasker won the Academy Award for Best Photography.

Krasker is remembered, if at all, as the black-and-white cameraman who had a notable influence on the American film-noir school, but his colour work was also impressive. *Henry V*, directed by Laurence Olivier in 1944, was filmed at a time when colour movies were at a relatively early stage of development. The fashion at the time was for bright, even lighting, a garish colour palette and excessive make-up on the actors. Krasker didn't hesitate to use contrast in his lighting (one of Olivier's soliloquies was filmed at dawn, despite the fervent objections of the Technicolor advisors) and he freed the bulky cameras of the period from the static images which had become their trademark. No one who has seen this superb film can forget the tracking shot which follows the French knights as they charge towards the English archers.

Other notable colour work by Krasker includes Visconti's *Senso* (1954), *Trapeze* (1956, directed by Carol Reed), and *El Cid* and *The Fall of the Roman Empire* (1961 and 1964, both directed by Anthony Mann).

Krasker became disenchanted with the growing amount of studio interference in films in the 1960s and this, allied with his deteriorating health, resulted in his retirement after Sidney Hayers' *The Trap* in 1966. Colleagues have commented on his modest, unassuming nature and his ability to collaborate with production designers and directors. Evidently he used his Academy Award as a doorstop in his Ealing house.

2010

Sven Nykvist: An Appreciation

Sven Nykvist was the son of missionaries who spent most of their time in the Belgian Congo. Born in 1922, he was brought up back in Sweden by relatives who were under instructions that young Sven was not to see movies because of the triple threat they presented in their endorsement of alcohol, tobacco and sex. Nothing, of course, is more alluring than the forbidden, so Sven studied photography, then joined the film industry in Stockholm in his late teens.

He worked his way up in the classic manner: from camera loader to focus puller and then camera operator.

He attracted the attention of the director Ingmar Bergman and was offered the position of director of photography on *The Virgin Spring* in 1960. I remember seeing the film in Sydney in that year and was astonished not only at the plotline—so startling among the tame tales of that era—of rape and revenge set in fourteenth-century Sweden, but of the striking black-and-white images, the flawlessly framed compositions and the startling close-ups which seemed to be delving into the thoughts of the characters.

Despite an allegedly tempestuous relationship with Bergman (evidently a characteristic of Bergman's working method), Nykvist went on to photograph at least another fifteen films for him, including the remarkable *Shame* (1968)—set in a bleak post-apocalyptic future—and *Persona* (1966), which switched from the wintry landscapes of so many Bergman films to an emphasis on huge sidelit close-ups of the two leading women, Bibi Andersson and Liv Ullmann. Nykvist's black-and-white camerawork was so accomplished, the lighting so natural and so beautiful without ever seeming to be striving for effect, that I assumed he avoided colour work out of an inability to master it. Yet he stunned with his use of saturated hues and the balance of tones in Bergman's *Autumn Sonata* (1978) and *Fanny and Alexander.*

Nykvist won the Academy Award for his photography of Bergman's *Cries and Whispers* (1972) and then again for *Fanny and Alexander.* The latter was made for television and the full version runs over four hours. The Edwardian period recreation is flawless and it's hard to think of another film where the interiors are such a delight to the eye. A change of style in some frightening dream sequences show that Nykvist was far more than a purely decorative lighting cameraman.

A relaxation of the union rules in America took Nykvist over there, where he shot films as varied as Louis Malle's *Pretty Baby* (1978) and Nora Ephron's *Sleepless in Seattle* (1993). He photographed a number of films for Woody Allen, a director with as good an eye for cameramen (he's used Carlo Di Palma and Gordon Willis too) as he has an ear for music. *Another Woman* (1988) and *Crimes and Misdemeanors* (1989) were both in colour but the severely underrated *Celebrity* (1998) was a triumphant return to the black-and-white photography with which he began his illustrious career.

I met Sven Nykvist a few times in London in the late 1980s, as we had a mutual friend in the designer Ken (later Sir Kenneth) Adam. He was tall, bearded, courteous and softly spoken. I wish I had been able to ask him more about his career with Ingmar Bergman, but his attention was diverted away from me to his attractive young woman companion—a characteristic, Ken Adam assured me, of Nykvist's entourage.

...

Sven Nykvist died in 2006.

2009

Don McAlpine, Cameraman

I first met Don McAlpine in 1972. I was going to direct my first feature film and had to find a cameraman. There had been very few feature films shot in Australia around that period, so I decided to look at a number of documentaries in the hope that I would be able to find and then interest someone.

It didn't take me long to realise that the best photographed ones were all done by the same person: Don McAlpine. I tracked Don down—he was working at the Commonwealth Film Unit—and suggested he throw in a steady job to shoot a raucous comedy that had only a four-week schedule with a first-time director. To my amazement, he agreed to what seemed to be a proposition fraught with danger.

Don was around thirty-nine at the time of the first Barry McKenzie film. A man of average height, he had blue eyes and ginger hair and beard. He had grown up in the country, I think in a town called Temora. I'd never heard of it. I still haven't. Don's dyslexia had limited his educational opportunities but he had made the most of a sturdy physique and became a physical-education instructor at a high school. He was a keen amateur photographer and sent in a number of local stories to ABC TV. These were so well photographed that he was invited to come to Sydney to work full-time as a professional cameraman for the news service.

Dyslexia, I've noticed, is not uncommon among great photographers. No doubt their skill develops in a visual direction, as the written word can be a meaningless jumble. Don had no problem whatever with numbers but usually confused left and right. Once he gave me elaborate directions to visit him and his wife, Jeanette, for lunch at their house somewhere outside Gosford, on the Central Coast. After scrupulously following his instructions, which I had written down as he dictated them over the phone, I found myself at the end of a bush track somewhere in the mountains. Locating a phone in a small town (this was all prior to mobile phones) I called Don, who immediately knew what the problem was. 'Just reverse everything I've told you,' he said. 'All the right turns are left and vice versa.' This worked. I arrived at the house in time for dinner.

Don did a wonderful job on the McKenzie film, especially considering the shooting was nearly all done in London in midwinter. The light bore no resemblance to light in Australia. A grey gloom emerged around 10 a.m. and it was dark again by 3 p.m. I remember Don looking at his exposure meter and saying, 'It's midday but I'm getting a reading of 1.9!'

The film was popular with Australian audiences but a critical disaster. In full kamikaze mode, I decided to make a sequel, *Barry McKenzie Holds His Own*. Don agreed to shoot it. Critical reaction was even worse and no one seemed to notice Don's superb photography, which this time included complicated split-screen effects (this was all before computer technology), as Barry Crocker played both McKenzie and his twin brother.

Luckily for me, my next project was *Don's Party*. Again, Don McAlpine's work was outstanding, especially as he had to shoot eleven actors in one small house throughout the entire film. Characteristically, he was inventive and amazingly fast. The camera was as big as a refrigerator but even that didn't faze him. Further, his amiable personality and respect for actors made my job a lot easier.

My next film was *The Getting of Wisdom*, an adaptation of the Henry Handel Richardson novel set mostly in a

Melbourne girls' school in 1898. I had been obsessed with this autobiographical story since finding an old paperback of the book in a London street market in 1965.

Executives at the Australian Film Commission were wary of Don doing the photography, as the story would clearly need a completely different visual style to the McKenzie films and *Don's Party*. I insisted he shoot the film, pointing out that he was an artist, not just a photographer, and would be capable of adapting his lighting style to the Victorian period setting of the new film. I was quite right. Although I've admired Don's work in the fifty or so films he has done since *The Getting of Wisdom*, it remains visually his most beautiful work. His candlelit interiors are ravishing, as are the scenes in the old school setting and in the Victorian houses, which he invariably lit with lights outside the windows, simulating a period in which there was either no electric light or the supply was through very low-wattage bulbs.

After that we went on to films such as *Breaker Morant*, *The Club* (1980), *Puberty Blues* and *The Fringe Dwellers* (1986). Every time, Don demonstrated astonishing artistry, his lighting varying to suit the subject matter—always, I think, the sign of a great cameraman. *Breaker Morant* was the film which catapulted both Don and myself to America, where we've each worked on a number of projects.

I looked up IMDb and saw that Don has now photographed fifty-five feature films and has worked with an array of leading directors—including Martin Ritt, Phillip Noyce, Chris Columbus, P. J. Hogan, Lee Tamahori, Ron Howard. Much of his career has been on American movies, but he still lives in his strange underground house near Gosford.

He hasn't forgotten Australia, either. His films include *Moulin Rouge* (2001), *Peter Pan* (2003) and the highly successful *The Dressmaker* (2015)—all works which demonstrate that, although now in his mid-eighties, Don has lost none of his legendary skill. He still seems to be very fit physically and, irritatingly, still has the ginger hair and beard, though there are a few streaks of grey, I was gratified to notice.

It has amazed me for years that the names of many outstanding still photographers are widely celebrated, yet equally gifted movie cameramen are unknown outside the film industry. I consider Don McAlpine to be in the front rank of these great artists.

2017

Ken Adam: A Personal Memoir

Ken Adam, who died on 10 March 2016, was a noted film production designer—perhaps the only one of the thousands who have designed the sets for films whose name has become known outside the film industry.

Ken was born Klaus Hugo Adam in Berlin on 5 December 1921. His parents, Lilli and Fritz Adam, were Jewish and owned a fashionable clothing store. Not surprisingly the rise of the Nazi party was regarded by the family with dismay. They moved to London in 1934. The family lived in Highgate, where Lilli ran a boarding house. Fritz, a proud ex-Prussian cavalryman from the First World War, fell into depression and never managed to cope with his sudden change of status—from a successful and admired businessman to refugee.

Ken was sent to the prestigious St Paul's School in London, took up cricket and embarked on the road to becoming an Englishman. Perhaps he arrived in England a little too late (he was fourteen) to ever entirely lose his German accent, which remained with him to the end of his long life.

His hatred of the Nazis led him to join the RAF in 1940. He flew a Hawker Typhoon on hundreds of missions over Germany until the war ended in 1945. Celebrated for his low-level attacks, he was known to his fellow pilots as Heinie the Tank-Buster. When King George VI visited the squadron all of the airmen were assembled for a greeting. The King passed along the line, asking each man where he was born. He was taken aback when Ken Adam replied, 'Berlin, sir.' After a moment the stunned King replied, 'Well, you're on the right side now.'

He studied architecture at the Bartlett School in London but appears to have abandoned the course to work as a draftsman on various film productions. He was associate art director to Paul Sheriff on *The Crimson Pirate* (1952), a popular swashbuckler with an athletic and eternally grinning Burt Lancaster. This was filmed in Ischia, near Naples. It was here that he met and married a local beauty, Maria Letizia Moauro.

Ken's first major credit as designer was on *Night of the Demon* (1957), a low-budget cult success directed by Jacques Tourneur. A big-budget but risible *Sodom and Gomorrah* (directed by Robert Aldrich) was a 1962 disaster but displayed such design flair that Ken was engaged for the first James Bond film, *Dr. No*, the same year. The producers realised that the immense success of this film was due in part to the style and inventiveness of the sets, so the relationship continued with *Goldfinger* (1964), *Thunderball* (1965), *You Only Live Twice* (1967) and *Diamonds Are Forever* (1971).

It was the designs for Stanley Kubrick's *Dr. Strangelove* (1964)—the war-room set in particular has been copied by architects worldwide—that lifted Ken Adam, production designer, to legendary status. Oddly, he did not collect an Academy Award for this but had to wait for Kubrick's *Barry Lyndon* (1975), where his period recreation remains unsurpassed to this day. Kubrick's obsession with detail drove Ken, another obsessive but clearly not in the same class, to a nervous breakdown. Despite an expressed fondness for and admiration of Kubrick, Ken avoided designing his later films.

A second Academy Award followed, with *The Madness of King George* (1994). He had a further three Academy nominations and won a BAFTA twice—for *The Ipcress File* (1965) and *Dr. Strangelove*. He had seven other BAFTA nominations.

I first worked with Ken in 1985, when he designed my disastrous biblical epic *King David*. The failure of this effort was in no way due to his powerful, realistic sets but to an inadequate script, some miscasting and my own stumbles as director.

We did far better together the following year with a film of Beth Henley's delightful play *Crimes of the Heart*. In contrast to all of the epics designed by Ken Adam this film was set almost entirely in one house. On a location survey in South Carolina we found an abandoned house in a small town, Southport. I had been told that Ken was imperious and non-collaborative but found this was not the case. We spent weeks discussing the script and worked out how the house could be used to make it visually interesting without letting it swamp the actors. Ken, always aware of the qualities of camera lenses, moved walls, changed sightlines, altered windows, added a tower and made sure every room was dressed meticulously to reflect the diverse personalities of the three sisters who lived uneasily together.

A couple of years later Ken designed an opera I directed in Spoleto, Puccini's *The Girl of the Golden West*. I told him I would like the barroom set and the mountain cabin to look as real as possible, as I thought this may be a way of pasting over the improbable plot and characterisations. This approach surprised him a little but, as always, he saw his designs fulfilling the concept of the director. The production was a triumph: the sets were enthusiastically applauded and went a long way to making up for the rather inadequate tenor and soprano.

I've had people tell me that Ken Adam was something of a snob, but I think they were misled by his grand house near Harrods in Knightsbridge, his passion for cigars and the white Rolls-Royce that he drove regally around London. I always found him to be amiable and unfailingly courteous—to everyone. A fanatically hard worker, nothing could distract him during the day as he did sketch after sketch, all skilfully drawn, for whatever film he was designing. In the evenings, the Knightsbridge house would be full of guests from all over Europe enjoying Ken and Letizia's hospitality and listening to Ken's anecdotes in English, French, Italian and German—the last not his favourite language.

Ken was knighted in 2003. When I last saw him, in 2012, he was arranging for his vast library of set designs—meticulously catalogued and stored over a seventy-year career covering over sixty films—to be sent to the Deutsche Kinemathek in Berlin. These will be of inestimable value to film historians and students but also, as some exhibitions have already demonstrated, fascinating to the general public.

His wife, Letizia, survives him. They had no children.

2016

Georges Delerue, Composer

Georges Delerue (1925–92) wrote the music for over 350 films and television productions. He was born near Lille and studied at the Conservatoire de Paris, supporting himself by playing the clarinet at weddings, funerals and dances, and in jazz bands. He began writing music for stage productions, then moved to films. He wrote scores for French, English and American directors. And one Australian.

I think that the first film score I ever heard by Georges Delerue was *Jules and Jim*, in the early 1960s. I was captivated by its melodic charm and the manner in which it captured the spirit of the movie. Today, the score has not dated at all, a claim that can be made for few films even ten years old, but this is a characteristic of all of Delerue's film music.

Through the 1960s, 1970s and into the 1980s, I continued to find Delerue's scores fascinating. Not just those for virtually all of the Truffaut films, but also movies such as Bertolucci's *The Conformist* (1970), with its invigorating jazz rhythms. At first I thought of him as best suited to comedies, probably because the Truffaut films were made with a gentle Gallic touch, but his gift for melody and enormous versatility were demonstrated with films such as *The Pumpkin Eater* (1964), *A Man for All Seasons* (1966), *Our Mother's House* (1967) and, in America, *Silkwood* (1983), *Salvador* (1986) and *Platoon* (1986). Every score he wrote fitted the film so perfectly. His understanding of story and character was so acute that his music always added depth and subtlety.

In the mid-1980s, Delerue began to spend months of each year in Los Angeles scoring American movies, and I decided to approach him about my film *Crimes of the Heart*. At this time, he spoke barely any English and we had to speak mostly through an interpreter. Any qualms I had about his understanding of the movie vanished on the first day of recording, when the first chords of his inventive but unmistakable style were played against the images of the film. Georges seemed charmed by *Crimes of the Heart*, which was uncommonly well-written by Beth Henley. I wanted him to capture the intimacy of the three sisters and the Southern ambiance. For the main title, a haunting ballad, Georges suggested the saxophone because one of the sisters, Sissy Spacek, plays it in one scene.

Over the next five years, Delerue scored another four of my films: his music for the comedy *Her Alibi* (1989) has some of the vivacity of the Truffaut scores while, regrettably, the film is not in the same class, although Georges' delightfully light and witty score made this rather dull film appear much better than it was. For *Mister Johnson* I asked him to write an English violin concerto and he produced one which Elgar would have been proud to write. There was another drama, set in Canada in 1630, *Black Robe*, and, finally the comedy-drama *Rich in Love* (1993), his last score, in which his music hit the exact tone we had never been able to find with any of the temporary tracks used for test screenings.

Georges Delerue's command of English improved (though it was always colourfully bizarre), to the point where we dispensed with the interpreter (my earnest study of French helped a little), but language was curiously unimportant to a man of so much instinctive human understanding, so much wit, so much charm. Every film he saw he appeared to comprehend immediately in every detail. If, during the editing, the most minor changes were made he would instantly notice. Even a major reshuffling of scenes appeared not to bother him. He would seemingly calmly and effortlessly rearrange the music cues to fit once again, as seamlessly as ever. He worked like a demon, with a brilliant flair for organisation that was obviously geared to give him as much time as possible to actually sit and write his beloved music.

Georges was the best organised person I've ever met. Every conducting session went like clockwork. If the start was 9 a.m., you could be sure his baton would be coming down for the first note exactly on time. He was courteous to the musicians, encouraging and appreciative. Every section of music was flawlessly prepared and always precisely fitted the scene. He invariably cleverly changed the orchestration during dialogue passages, so that the music never struggled against the words.

From a human point of view, Georges was very kind by nature, very amiable—I never saw him lose his temper even to a minor degree—and had that relaxed manner that I tend to associate, perhaps naively, with my French friends. He was intensely musical and appeared to know absolutely everything about music, every note from every composer from every country in the world. Due to his flawless management of time every appointment was kept; every piece of music was ready exactly when he said it would be; every recording session worked precisely as he predicted it would. Yet he did all this with no apparent effort and with total affability.

During my career I've collaborated with many gifted

composers but Georges will always be my favourite. Today, when I look at old films of his on television, I am captivated all over again by his music. It never seems to date and always enhances the mood. He could go from comedies to drama with equal skill. I think his music for *Black Robe* is one of the greatest film scores ever written—so much of the film is without dialogue that it was left to the images and music to convey mood and character.

As well as film scores, Georges wrote numerous classical pieces (he had trained with Darius Milhaud) that fascinatingly reveal a darker side to his personality. They reject the easy melody of his film music and the lightness of touch characteristic of French composers and seem influenced by Bartók and the East European school.

Georges Delerue was a small and somewhat misshapen man because of a childhood spinal deformity. He had a huge head and a thick mane of blond hair. Despite his ungainly appearance I always imagined he was tremendously attractive to women. He was greatly loved by all who knew him, all of whom will always miss him.

2009

Erich Korngold: A Sketch

Erich Wolfgang Korngold was born in 1897 in Brünn, Moravia, but his family moved to Vienna in 1901, when Erich's father, Julius, took over as music critic for the *Neue Freie Presse*, a position he held until 1934.

Erich was a child prodigy. A Berlin professor of music wrote to Julius Korngold, 'your son is phenomenal even among the exceptional cases of early music development.' The sentiment was echoed by Mahler, who was so impressed by young Erich's cantata *Gold* in 1906 that he immediately arranged for him to study with Alexander

Zemlinsky. Richard Strauss was another admirer of his youthful works—a piano trio, a piano sonata and a ballet, *The Snowman*, which was performed for Emperor Franz Joseph when Erich was eleven years old.

Two one-act operas, *Violanta* and *Der Ring des Polykrates*, preceded Korngold's first full-length opera, *Die Tote Stadt* (The Dead City), which premiered simultaneously in Hamburg and Cologne in 1920. It was also the first opera from Austria or Germany to be performed after the First World War at the Metropolitan in New York, where the lush scoring and melodic invention were as acclaimed as they were in Europe.

Erich Korngold and his father collaborated on the libretto (though Julius Korngold wrote under a pseudonym and his involvement was only revealed after his death), which was adapted from the novel *Bruges-la-Morte*, written by Georges Rodenbach and first published in France in 1892. The libretto follows the novel reasonably faithfully but, no doubt because of the influence of often impenetrable Viennese psychiatric theories, continues the story past the death by strangulation of Marietta (which ends the novel) and reveals a world of dreams and delusion.

During the 1920s Erich Korngold wrote another opera, *Das Wunder der Heliane* (The Miracle of Heliane), which was not as well received as *Die Tote Stadt*, apart from favourable reviews by Julius Korngold, but which Erich Korngold always regarded as his greatest operatic achievement. Performances have been rare for the last ninety years of a work described as—even by the standards of opera librettos—having 'a particularly ludicrous and symbolically overloaded plot'. Recently, some of its splendid arias have been recorded by Renée Fleming.

Korngold also wrote a charming piano concerto for the left hand specifically for the pianist Paul Wittgenstein (brother of the unintelligible philosopher), who had lost his right arm during the First World War. Wittgenstein, a famously difficult personality, was critical, just as he was of the concertos he commissioned from Hindemith, Prokofiev, Ravel, Strauss and Britten.

In an effort to achieve financial stability and against the advice of his father, Korngold arranged and conducted some of the forgotten operettas of Johann Strauss II, among them *A Night in Venice* and *Cagliostro in Vienna*. This led, perhaps not surprisingly, to a revival of interest in these lightweight works.

In the early 1930s Korngold was invited to Hollywood by Max Reinhardt to arrange Mendelssohn's music for a film version of *A Midsummer Night's Dream*, with a cast that included James Cagney, Olivia de Havilland, Joe E. Brown, Mickey Rooney (!) and Dick Powell. The film, which is elaborate, bizarre and well worth watching, was not a success but brought Korngold to the notice of Los Angeles producers. A couple of years later, with Hitler on the path to power and the Jewish community high on the hit list, he accepted an invitation from Warner Bros. to move his family to California.

Between 1934 and 1946 he wrote the music for eighteen films, not a huge number compared with his fellow Viennese Max Steiner (1888–1971), who often composed the music for fifteen in one year. Korngold set the style for film music with a touch so definitive that it continues to this day. He wrote themes for the key characters, for locations and situations, and pioneered the use of music under dialogue to reinforce mood. He insisted on only scoring films from scripts he approved, kept copyright on his music and reserved the right to reuse his themes in classical compositions.

His first characteristically lushly orchestrated and melodic score was for *Captain Blood* (1935), though he curiously received no screen credit. He won an Academy Award for *Anthony Adverse* (1936) and for *The Adventures of Robin Hood* (1938). Other notable scores were written for *The Sea Hawk* (1940), *Kings Row* (1942) and *Deception* (1946).

Julius Korngold, never happy with his son's career as a composer for movies, died, aged eighty-five, in 1945. Prompted by this and by the end of the war, Erich Korngold returned to Vienna. He was shocked not just to see a ruined city, but to realise he was a forgotten figure whose music was considered to be from another era. After a few disappointing and poorly attended performances, he returned to America.

Erich Korngold's post-war works include a cello concerto, a violin concerto and a symphony. All of them used themes from his film scores and none were well received critically prior to his death, in 1957, but they are now frequently performed and recorded. The opera *Die Tote Stadt* has been staged successfully in Germany, the Czech Republic, Italy, England, America and Australia in recent years.

2011

IV

Opera, Painters, Writers

A Brief Guide to American Opera

The popularity of American musicals for the past hundred years has helped to obscure, even to the point of invisibility, the achievements of American opera composers. Everyone has heard the names of Rodgers and Hart, Rodgers (again) and Hammerstein, Lerner and Loewe, Victor Herbert (who wrote a failed opera, *Natoma*, in 1911), Kander and Ebb, Sondheim, Berlin, Gershwin and many more—yet most would struggle to name even three American operatic composers: Barber, Menotti (?), Floyd (??).

For this amazing array of talent we can thank, if

indirectly, the Russian tsar and his late-nineteenth-century pogroms, which drove so many talented Russian Jews to emigrate to America, where they, or their sons, quickly came to dominate and enervate Broadway.

The difference between a musical and an opera is difficult to define, adding confusion. In general, musicals have more in common with the traditional European operettas of composers such as Lehar, Kalman and Offenbach. They tend to have slight stories with loads of titled characters, are dramatically undemanding yet packed with 'luscious melody, rousing choruses and romantic passions'. There is often dialogue, invariably inane, to carry the plot along between the musical numbers—while very few operas have any dialogue at all. The technical demands made on singers in operettas are considerable, as they invariably are with 'serious' opera. This is not always the case with musicals. Definite non-singers such as Rex Harrison (*My Fair Lady*), Jonathan Pryce (*Miss Saigon*) and Jean Simmons (*A Little Night Music*) have made a huge success of their roles, in much as the same way as so many pop stars have overcome non-existent musical ability with presentation and presence, even charisma. (Although it seems to me that in the pop world celebrity can be achieved even if all three factors are absent.)

Most of the great nineteenth-century operas were performed in America from the 1830s onwards, when Lorenzo Da Ponte was instrumental in building New

York's first Italian opera house. (Having written librettos for Mozart, he later became a bankrupt and in 1805 emigrated to New York, where he opened a grocery store!) They were usually pirated versions presented in a truncated form, rearranged and even retitled, no doubt with the intention of avoiding litigation from the composers. By the end of the century a number of American-born composers had tried their hand at grand opera. All failed. Few had the panache of William Henry Fry, whose *Leonora* (1845) was a disaster. 'I like to hear hissing,' he said. 'No artiste is good for anything until he is soundly hissed.'

During the reign of the celebrated Giulio Gatti-Casazza as director of the Metropolitan Opera (1910–35), seventeen new American operas were premiered. None were successful and none have been resuscitated. It is unlikely ever to happen as the names—of both the operas and composers—have nearly all been forgotten. This is perhaps not too surprising. How many of the numerous operas of *King Lear* are performed today? Much of the standard fare of the world's opera houses remains the province of a small number of nineteenth-century composers—predominantly Italian—of genius: Verdi, Donizetti, Bellini, Rossini. (Puccini, who died in 1926, is essentially a nineteenth-century composer, most of his librettos being drawn from Victorian melodramas.) However, the vast majority of nineteenth-century operas have vanished, although the odd one re-emerges and creeps into the repertoire. Rossini's charming *La Cenerentola* (1817) began to reappear in the 1930s, having had very few performances after Rossini's death in 1868, and is now staged worldwide with regularity.

The story of contemporary opera is similar. A large number of works have been written, had one or two performances and not been heard again. Some composers, such as Mascagni, had one huge hit—in his case, *Cavalleria Rusticana*, first performed in 1884—and then spent a lifetime trying to create another. The twentieth-century composers with the most works in the world's opera houses are Strauss and Britten, though Janáček now seems to have a foot firmly in the door. By these criteria, the number of American operas being performed—mostly in America, admittedly—is respectable, especially considering they have to overcome considerable prejudice against the home-grown product and also deal with the curious resistance opera audiences have to new works. If film and theatre audiences had to see the same films and plays repeatedly, cinemas and theatres would soon be empty.

...

The first American opera to show undoubted staying power is George Gershwin's *Porgy and Bess* (1935), though the debate is still raging about whether it is an opera at all and not just an uncommonly well-written musical conceived for operatic voices. The matter hardly seems worth debating.

Whatever it is, it is a masterpiece, and its appeal seems universal. Gershwin is undeniably a composer of genius. Probably the sheer popularity of his songs for theatre and movies (with lyrics by his brother Ira) has been responsible for some critics dismissing him as a lightweight, in much the same way as snobbish critics have dismissed the verse of John Betjeman on the grounds that anything so immensely popular couldn't possibly have any merit.

Porgy and Bess had a revival in London in 2006, stylishly directed by Trevor Nunn. This was staged in a revised version with dialogue from the original novel by DuBose Heyward, but with the music intact though re-orchestrated for a smaller orchestra. The original 1935 production—incredibly, not particularly well received by critics of the time—was revised a number of times by Gershwin, making the choice of a definitive version highly problematic. Many of the most celebrated operas have survived with lame librettos but superb music; *Porgy and Bess*, though benefiting from a score in which every song has become a standard, makes a good case for the advantages of a strong storyline and detailed characters.

...

The most acclaimed 'serious' opera composer working in America, at least during the 1940s and 1950s, was Gian Carlo Menotti. He was born in Italy in 1911 but studied in

America from 1928. His first opera, *Amelia Goes to the Ball*, was performed at the Met in 1936. A string of successes followed, all with highly original librettos written by Menotti himself, the majority of them set in the twentieth century and made accessible to audiences by his use of traditional harmonies. *The Medium* (1945), about a fraudulent spiritualist, ran for eight months and was accompanied by a short comic work, 'The Telephone'. His first full-length opera, *The Consul* (1949), a Kafka-influenced tale of people trying to get visas to leave an unnamed police state, also had an eight-month run and won the Pulitzer and the Drama Critics' Circle Award. It has been performed worldwide in at least ten languages. Menotti's Christmas opera *Amahl and the Night Visitors* was written for television in 1951, was a huge hit and was regularly revived for decades. It's difficult to imagine any network commissioning an opera today.

After *The Saint of Bleecker Street* (which won another Pulitzer) in 1954, Menotti had less success with opera, though his numerous orchestral compositions—which include a piano and violin concerto and a superb cantata, *The Death of the Bishop of Brindisi*—also show his melodic flair and deserve far more performances and recordings. It is likely his involvement with the Spoleto Festival, inaugurated in 1958, took up far too much of his creative time. His last opera, *Goya* (1986), was an ambitious failure, despite the presence of Placido Domingo in the eponymous role. Frail but alert, Menotti lived in his Scottish castle rather like a character from one of his own early librettos until his death in 2007, in his mid-nineties.

...

Carlisle Floyd, born in 1926 in South Carolina, is almost unique among opera composers in that he has concentrated on that form alone, an example of singular dedication which must have been frequently dispiriting. Working as his own librettist and frequently drawing on life in the Southern states—which he knows so well—he has created an impressive series of works, the best known of which, *Susannah*, premiered in 1955, although it didn't make it to the Met for another thirty years. A retelling, set in the Appalachian Mountains (and complete with the dialect of that region), of the biblical story of Susannah and the Elders, its popularity hasn't waned—there have been over two hundred productions to date. One of the arias, 'Ain't It a Pretty Night', is a favourite in recital programmes all over the world.

With a style described by Grove as 'eclectic, conservative, well-crafted and stageworthy', Floyd has continued to produce opera after opera, every one of them dramatically gripping and musically thrilling. *Of Mice and Men* (1970), from the Steinbeck novel, has been performed in European houses as well as having innumerable American productions. Other works include *Wuthering Heights* (1958), *Willie Stark* (1981) and *Cold Sassy Tree*, a characteristically melodic work with vivid characterisations, the world premiere of which I was privileged to direct for Houston Grand Opera in 2001.

...

The other major figure of American opera is undoubtedly Samuel Barber (1910–81), best known for his appealing violin, piano and cello concertos and three sublime song cycles. His 'Adagio for Strings' (actually the slow movement of his String Quartet) is known worldwide from its use in the film *Platoon*. Barber's operatic reputation consists of two works, *Vanessa* (1958) and *Antony and Cleopatra* (1966). *Vanessa*, with a libretto by Barber's 'partner' Gian Carlo Menotti, from a typically gothic Isak Dinesen story, premiered at the Met (with Eleanor Steber, Rosalind Elias and Giorgio Tozzi) and was an immediate success—which didn't stop Barber revising it considerably. It has subsequently been staged in numerous European as well as American houses—although not yet in Australia—and has been described as 'by far the finest and most truly "operatic" opera ever written by an American, as well as one of the most impressive things of its sort to appear anywhere since Richard Strauss's more vigorous days'.

The praise heaped on *Vanessa* created high expectations for *Antony and Cleopatra*, commissioned for the opening of the new Metropolitan Opera House, Lincoln Center, in 1966. Franco Zeffirelli was the director. The first-night audience, and then the critics, castigated the production as over-elaborate and the music as disappointing. Barber was shattered by the failure; with true operatic panache he became an alcoholic and then died of cancer.

I saw the Spoleto revival in 1986, and it was hard to imagine what prompted the 1966 antipathy. Even in a poorly directed production (by Menotti, who could compose and write librettos but was, at best, an indifferent director), the sensuous music was immediately appealing in both melody and orchestration. At least three of the arias—'Give Me Some Music', 'Give Me My Robe, Put On My Crown, I Have Immortal Longings in Me' and 'Oh Take, Oh Take Those Lips Away' (the last added by Barber when revising the work)—are among the highlights of the entire opera repertoire and stand comparison with the finest achievements of the acknowledged masters. No revival of *Antony and Cleopatra* has succeeded in establishing the work. I find it hard to believe that this will not happen soon.

...

More recent operas by John Adams (born 1947) and Philip Glass (born 1937) have been quite widely performed. Both are leading minimalist composers, though neither has eschewed lyricism. Their works are surprisingly melodic, quite unlike, say, those of Michael Tippett or Harrison

Birtwistle, both of whom subject their audiences to an ordeal rather than an entertainment. Part of the appeal has been due, no doubt, to the vagaries of fashion. Both Glass and Adams have been promoted as ultra-modern and the nature of their operas—Glass's *Akhnaten* from 1983, for example, is sung in Egyptian, Akkadian and Hebrew—takes them out of what is perceived as the stuffy realm of conventional opera to the level of a theatrical experience. Yet, despite all the hype and acclaim, both are accomplished and highly gifted composers.

Key works by Adams are *Nixon in China* (1987) and *The Death of Klinghoffer* (1991). Apart from *Akhnaten*, Glass's best known operas are *Einstein on the Beach* (1976) and *The Voyage* (1992), the latter commissioned for the five-hundredth anniversary of the arrival of Columbus in America. It is an idiosyncratic work, with fine choral writing, in which Glass managed to include a figure reminiscent of Stephen Hawking.

...

Other American composers have written one or two works which have maintained their popularity at least in their country of origin. Douglas Moore's *The Ballad of Baby Doe*, first performed in 1958, approaches musical-comedy territory. It is based on a true story about a Colorado silver miner and is a feast of ballads, waltzes and dance-hall tunes. Robert

Ward (born 1917), an army-band director during the Second World War, has written six operas, only one of which, *The Crucible* (1961), derived from the Arthur Miller play about the Salem witch trials, receives occasional stagings. I directed this powerful work at the Kennedy Center in Washington some years ago. Its melodies evoke seventeenth-century Protestant hymns and I can't imagine that it would fail to impress audiences anywhere in the world. In fact, the music adds an emotional punch that is somewhat lacking in the original play, which seems didactic by today's standards.

...

The prolific and gifted Stephen Sondheim (born 1930) is known for a number of musicals, at least two of which—*A Little Night Music*, 1973; and *Sweeney Todd: The Demon Barber of Fleet Street*, 1979—have made it onto the stages of a number of opera houses around the world. (Sydney audiences were thrilled by an imaginative Gale Edwards version of *Sweeney Todd* in 2001.)

Although he began his career as a lyricist of uncommon verbal dexterity (for *West Side Story* in 1957 and *Gypsy* in 1959), he began to write the music as well, with *A Funny Thing Happened on the Way to the Forum* (1962). His style is accessible—trivial, it is often claimed by spoilsports—combining jazz and dance idioms along with influences from Debussy and Ravel.

. . .

The almost ludicrously talented (pianist, conductor, composer) Leonard Bernstein has written a number of operas cum operettas cum Broadway musicals—*West Side Story* is easily the best known, but *Candide* is more adventurous and more exciting musically. It premiered in 1956, directed by the legendary Tyrone Guthrie, and was an unexpected and resounding flop, despite delightful tunes, a witty book (Hugh Wheeler) and even wittier lyrics (Richard Wilbur and Sondheim). Directors have remained loyal to it over the years, through numerous revisions. Their determination has resulted in a painfully gradual increase it its popularity, despite regular critical maulings.

. . .

Back in the world of undeniably serious opera, the Florida-born (1961) composer Jake Heggie has made an impact with *Dead Man Walking* (1998)—based on the movie of the same name—about a man on death row. A gloomy subject, but tragedy is so often the *raison d'être* of the opera world, as happy endings are symptomatic of the film industry. The Australian (New Zealand?) singer Teddy Tahu Rhodes has performed with great success in this work and also, with Cheryl Barker, in Heggie's *The End of the Affair* (2004), adapted from the bittersweet Graham Greene novel.

. . .

A Streetcar Named Desire—music by André Previn and libretto by Philip Littell—is the most instantly successful American opera since Menotti's *The Consul.* It has already had numerous revivals in both America and Europe since its San Francisco premiere (with Renée Fleming and Rodney Gilfry) in 1998. Tennessee Williams' steamy, exotic plays, which draw their characters from his own inexhaustibly dysfunctional family, all seem to be ideal opera material, and Previn and Littell made the most of their opportunity.

Although it has less jazz influence (perhaps that would have been a cliché) than I would have expected from a noted jazz pianist, the score is atmospheric and dramatic, with at least two show-stopping soprano arias. (Previn's recording of the opera won the Grand Prix du Disque.) Still, it is not an entirely satisfying work. Only the soprano role (Blanche DuBois) is given a number of arias, while both the baritone and tenor roles are minimal. Oddly, there is no trio for the key characters, an opportunity that would not have been overlooked by Benjamin Britten.

Streetcar is the culmination of Previn's astonishing career. Born in Germany in 1929, he and his family wisely moved to America to escape Hitler's lunacy. Settling in Los Angeles, he studied with the Italian composer Mario Castelnuovo-Tedesco—who was on the run from Mussolini. Previn was arranging music for MGM films and playing in a jazz combo at the age of nineteen. He won four Academy Awards—*Gigi*, 1958; *Porgy and Bess*, 1959; *My Fair Lady*, 1964; and *Thoroughly Modern Millie*, 1967—before deciding he wanted to pursue his classical career. (He covers his Hollywood years in an entertaining autobiography, *No Minor Chords*, published in 1991.)

Since then he has conducted major orchestras all over the world, including a long stint with the London Symphony, where he emerged as an unlikely but dynamic advocate of the symphonies of Vaughan Williams and Elgar. As well as marrying more than his share of beautiful women, including Mia Farrow and Anne-Sophie Mutter, Previn has made hundreds of recordings, either as conductor or pianist or both, yet still found time to write a number of song cycles, as well as a piano concerto for Vladimir Ashkenazy and a violin concerto for his (now ex-) wife, Anne-Sophie Mutter.

2007

Smart Lessons

It is probably not too great an exaggeration to say that I owe my entire appreciation of art to Jeffrey Smart. Growing up in the west of Sydney, with parents who were struggling for solvency in the years after the war, I had virtually no acquaintance with paintings or drawings of any description. We had no art books, except for Norman Lindsay's illustrations to *The Magic Pudding*. There was, I admit, a reproduction of a painting of cows at dawn by Elioth Gruner in the living room, about which I managed to be constantly and unquestionably irritatingly disparaging.

(Years later I admired it when I saw the original in a gallery. At least I learnt that reproductions have the capacity to trivialise excellent works.)

I recall only one school excursion to an art gallery, perhaps around 1953. I did not regard this as an exciting prospect, except that it meant a day free of lessons. The Art Gallery of New South Wales was, in those days, a sombre structure in which everyone tiptoed around and spoke in whispers. The Drysdale paintings of outback towns impressed me. I could feel the heat and dust. I was most taken, though, by Poynter's massive *Queen of Sheba Visiting King Solomon*, or some such absurd title. Here, I thought, was a man who could draw, who had technique (as did Drysdale) and could create beautiful and complex compositions. Perhaps a couple of partially clad young ladies in the composition added to the allure.

In the late 1950s I was working as an assistant in the newsreel department of the ABC. As I was young and strong, it was my job to load and unload the mountain of heavy equipment we seemed to need for the simplest interview—equipment that today, in the digital age, has been scrapped or is in a museum. Few celebrities seemed to visit Australia in that era and I have no recollection of those numerous trips to the airport resulting in anyone even faintly interesting chatting away onto our black-and-white 16 mm film. It might be salutary now to check the ABC archives, assuming any of the material was kept, to see just how many fascinating people appeared of whom I, full of teenage arrogance, was totally ignorant.

Apart from a few boring days at the cricket, where I was left to man the camera while the cameraman (Tom Ditcham, long dead, so I can state the name) adjourned to the bar, my only vivid memory of my assisting years was being sent to cover an art show, somewhere down near Circular Quay, by the painter Jeffrey Smart.

I remembered Jeffrey as being the art master at my school (King's). I had assumed—with no foundation, I suppose—that he was teaching art because he wasn't really an artist himself, in the same way that people teach screenwriting and film directing because they admire these skills rather than practise them or, more likely, were dismal failures when they attempted to practise them.

Jeffrey's paintings struck me so forcefully that I managed to black out almost one-third of the city by connecting our photographic lights into the wrong sockets. At least this gave me more time to study the paintings—the compositions, lighting and colours of which made the first impact. These were factors that I was not unaware of in movies. Being obsessed with that art form then (as now), I had spent all of my teenage years chasing around Sydney cinemas—Watsons Bay (a steam train from Toongabbie, where I lived, then a tram from Central Station), Cronulla, Wilberforce—to study the work of directors and cameramen I admired. The latter category included many great artists skilled in lighting and composition whose names deserve far greater recognition: Robert Krasker, who photographed *The Third Man*; Ted McCord—*Treasure of the Sierra Madre* (1948); Harry Stradling—*Carnival in Flanders* (1935) and *A Streetcar Named Desire* (1951); Georges Périnal—*The Fallen Idol* (1948); Gregg Toland—*The Grapes of Wrath* (1940) and *Citizen Kane* (1942).

Apart from his sheer technical skill, his sense of composition and light, I was stunned at that exhibition in 1959 by Jeffrey's subject matter—just as I am today. I continue to marvel at his inventiveness, his inexhaustible variations on his vision. I had always thought of painters in terms of rural scenes, historical scenes or portraits. Now I was confronted by someone who painted the world around him. He saw beauty in highways, buildings, road signs, factories and so on, just as the Heidelberg School had seen it in the rustic Australia of their time, and the Impressionists had painted the France which was a part of their everyday lives.

I never much cared for interpretations of Jeffrey's paintings which characterised the few human figures in them as lonely, alienated. It seemed to me they were included to give scale to the compositions. Why, I thought, if someone is alone on the balcony of a tower block is he necessarily unhappy? He's probably just admiring the view for a few minutes before going back inside to a G&T.

The filmmaker in me finds the narrative aspect of his paintings intriguing. It occurred to me a couple of years ago that one could present stage plays based on the paintings. The four men standing by a truck, for example: this image could be projected, actors could take the poses and then a story could be constructed which either begins or ends with the painting. Is the man in the foreground, hands on hips, demanding something of the others? Has there been a dispute? Over women? The right to drive certain routes?

The man in orange outside the garage (actually a portrait of me) in orange overalls. Has he lost his job? Is he waiting for someone? A wife? Girlfriend? Who?

That well-dressed middle-aged couple standing by the old billboard. Have they said something disquieting to the couple in the distance? Are they regretting what they've said? The departing couple certainly don't look happy.

...

My friendship with Jeffrey Smart began in 1963 when we found ourselves on the *Castel Felice*, sailing to Europe. This friendship continues to be one of the great joys of my life and, despite film work which has taken me all over the world, often for lengthy stays in improbable countries such as Nigeria and Bulgaria, I have made every effort to visit Jeffrey as often as possible. Twice in 2009 my wife, Virginia, and I visited him at his house near Arezzo in Tuscany, where I was able to watch as he completed some of the paintings for his next exhibition. Despite his advanced age, he worked for a few hours every day in his studio, meticulously adding detail to his canvases or doing innumerable studies, usually in oil but with freer brushwork than the final version. These studies enable him to work out the complex compositions. Once this is done he 'can finish the details—that's a breeze and doesn't take so long'.

He doesn't mind chatting while he paints, but adheres rigorously to his work schedule. (Correction! Jeffrey tells me he never talks to anyone while painting—with the exception of his colleague Ermes De Zan and myself.) Paintings with the painstaking detail of a Smart cannot be knocked off with a few Cy Twombly-type swishes of a brush or the spilled-pots-of-paint effect of Pollock and his followers.

The day's work over, a sociable Jeffrey emerges. Visitors often arrive for dinner on the verandah. The conversation is usually laced with salacious and delicious gossip, which my fabled discretion forbids me to repeat—though I am tempted to relate the details of the discussion regarding the length of Sibelius's virile member.

Before bed there could be a movie. Someone recently sent Jeffrey a box set of Marlene Dietrich's films of the 1930s, most of which I find highly resistible. Jeffrey watches her with intense fascination and can do a reasonable imitation, lisp and all, of her singing 'Go 'way from my window.' Jeffrey's friends all know him as a man with the wit of Whistler, plus an extensive knowledge of all the arts. He is one of those annoying people who, despite a formidable workload, seems to have read everything. He can quote T. S. Eliot's *Four Quartets* by heart and seems to have total recall of the most arcane plot twists of the novels of Anthony Trollope.

A visit to a gallery in his company is a revelation, as his knowledge reveals hidden depths of the painter in question, his technique and his subject matter. I've seen it written that Jeffrey is no admirer of abstract art of any period but I don't believe this to be true. His objections and reservations are to the many parvenu practitioners of this genre. I have heard him enthuse at length on the genius of both Ben Nicholson and Kandinsky.

Perhaps my most exciting visit with Jeffrey, though, was our trip to Liverpool around 2004 to a huge retrospective of Lawrence Alma-Tadema, the painter of vast historical subjects frequently with an ancient Roman setting. From a period of acclaim in the Edwardian era, Alma-Tadema's paintings declined in value through critical scorn until they were almost worthless. Dozens of them were collected, as a joke, by the curiously and unfortunately named American, Allen Funt, who found himself the owner of a goldmine when the pictures appreciated again in value.

It was a revelation going from one Alma-Tadema painting to another as Jeffrey, captivated by the sheer technical skill exhibited, could point to a detail and say: 'See… the hand, so hard to get it right from that perspective. He's rubbed it out and done it again and again.' 'Do you know,' he said, 'how he drew all the figures so flawlessly?' I didn't know: I thought he was just good. He was, but 'he drew them all nude in the studies so that he would know how the clothes draped on the body.'

Jeffrey studied with Fernand Léger in Paris and recently commented to me that he is sure Léger will one day 'be more acclaimed, and recognised as a greater painter than Picasso'.

I've noticed that many painters are more contemptuous of their contemporaries than film directors tend to be of theirs, although my dislike of the works of Hitchcock (couldn't direct actors) and Kubrick (terminally pretentious) is certainly regarded as bizarre. Jeffrey is certainly no slouch in dismissing a number of living or recently living painters who are misguidedly universally acclaimed. I find I'm inclined to agree with most of his views. And why shouldn't he have firm opinions? Critics do.

Not everyone is dismissed. Jeffrey greatly admires the work of Lucian Freud and the little-known Horace Trenerry, among others. His great passions, all the same—apart from Cézanne—are the Italian masters, particularly Piero della Francesca. Prints of Piero's work adorn the walls of Jeffrey's studio and he frequently visits the sublime murals by Piero in a church in Arezzo. He sent Virginia and me off on a tour around Tuscany and Umbria seeking out the works of Piero in various galleries and churches.

A shared interest in classical music was always a bond

between us. I have a vivid memory of Jeffrey in his studio painting away, the classical station blaring away at a terrific volume and Jeffrey complaining, 'Why don't they play more Delius? Bruce, can you get in touch with them and ask?'

I can't share his passion for Wagner, despite valiant efforts. Jeffrey, even in his eighties, tramples the globe to see and hear the Ring Cycle. I, on the other hand, admit there are sublime moments but can't cope with the extraordinary length or the absurd librettos which Wagner himself admitted he couldn't understand, as he'd borrowed them from so many diverse sources.

I am lucky that my career as a film and opera director has taken me around the world and into contact with many remarkable people. Jeffrey Smart is undoubtedly one of the most remarkable, also one of the kindest and most gifted. His paintings give me the same thrill today as they did at that exhibition in 1959.

...

Jeffrey Smart died in 2013.

2010

A Memory of Margaret Olley

I only met Margaret Olley somewhere towards the end of her long life, perhaps around eight to ten years before she died. I can't remember how we met, although I vividly recall my first visit, with my wife, to her house in Paddington. It was a lunch party, the first of many that I attended. I remember being struck by the astonishingly crowded room, packed with furniture, paintings, dried flowers and bric-a-brac picked up from numerous trips. Other guests lurked among the debris while Margaret cooked, a cigarette in her mouth, in the phone-booth-sized kitchen. Closer inspection revealed that this tiny space also seemed to be where she preferred to paint, as it held an easel, paints and a partially finished canvas.

I was always apprehensive that one of Margaret's ubiquitous cigarettes would result in a conflagration. That house, dry and savannah-like, would be cinders within a few minutes. Luckily, this never happened and Margaret, dismissing the advice of doctors and friends, smoked to the very end.

Once lunch was ready, the guests, usually about ten people, would sit around a dining-room table which had dried flowers, ancient dried flowers, lying along the centre. At a party some time after this first one, a guest whispered to me, with a tone of horror, that he had discovered a nest of mice happily frolicking among the dried leaves in the centre of the table.

Even when I first met Margaret she had a walking frame. In fact, I never saw her without it and had to look at photographs or the famous painting of her by Dobell to visualise a young Margaret. She may have looked old and may have moved with difficulty but her mind was sharp until the end of her life. She was witty and forthright, but somehow never offensive. Maybe it was just the case that those she offended weren't to be met at her lunch parties, but I don't recall anyone else I have met who was so widely liked, admired, loved. Perhaps Horton Foote was in that category, but I can think of no others.

She was free of narcissism and did not spend time discussing her work or her importance. She did not dominate the conversation, although she contributed vigorously. She was extraordinarily well-informed—not just about painters and painting, but music and literature. She was interested in others and was a generous and loyal friend. Only a short time before Margaret died, Virginia had a small party at a bookshop in Leichhardt for the launch of her new novel. She invited Margaret, not really thinking she could make it. But she did. On this occasion I remember asking her what she thought of the biography of her which had recently been published. 'Oh, that woman,' she said, referring to the author. 'She's obsessed with sex.'

The aspect of Margaret's personality that made the most impression on me was her work ethic. She painted every day. By the time I met her she could no longer travel with ease—although I recall that she and an equally elderly Jeffrey Smart visited the Louvre not too many years ago, which resulted in a superb portrait of Margaret by Jeffrey—so she turned her vast talent to painting the interior of her own cluttered house in Paddington. Beautiful paintings, superb in their use of colour and composition, and—amazingly—never repetitive.

In the last months of her life she somehow managed to get herself to Barry Humphries' apartment, where she sat on a tiny balcony and painted characteristically cheerful and vivid pictures of Sydney Harbour. Perhaps her pictorialism is out of fashion these days, but I'm inclined to agree with her views on art. After a visit to a gallery where an acclaimed artist was having an exhibition of his largely blank canvases, punctuated by an occasional black blob or straight line, Margaret looked at me and said, 'Nobody's home, dear, nobody's home.'

...

Margaret Olley died in 2011.

2011

Forgotten—and in Mildura

There was no direct flight from Sydney to Mildura when I decided to visit. 'There usta be,' one of the locals told me, helpfully. No train, either. 'There usta be'—same local.

Mildura is a twelve-hour drive from Sydney: over the mountains, through gently hilly pastureland, then, for the final three hours, through flat, featureless semi-desert country. There are occasional small towns, mostly with boarded-up shopfronts because of the drift to cities or larger rural towns. In the far west of New South Wales there is often a sign announcing a town, then a tiny abandoned church, then another sign bidding the driver farewell.

Mildura, on the Murray River in Victoria near the South Australian border, is a different story. Despite a few boarded-up shops, it seems quite prosperous: tree-lined streets, cafes, a bookshop. There are paddle steamers and houseboats on the river. The camping ground on the riverbank, among the gum trees, is full of holidaymakers. The river is full of them, too, as the temperature is 40 degrees Celsius in the sun.

Apart from tourism, this remote town is sustained by vineyards and olive plantations for oil. The object of my visit, though, was one of the world's most remote art galleries, the Mildura Arts Centre, which was having an exhibition of paintings and drawings by Frank Brangwyn (1867–1956) and William Orpen (1878–1931), two virtually forgotten painters—English and Irish, respectively—once collected by the Australian R. D. Elliott (1884–1950) and left to the town of Mildura, 'provided a gallery was built to house them'.

...

I became aware of the work of Brangwyn in the mid-1990s, when I went to an exhibition at the Royal Academy of Arts in London of 'paintings from regional galleries'. Almost all the paintings on display were of the technically assured figurative school of the 1890–1940 period that appeals to me, no matter how often I am assured by my children and various otherwise astute friends that this work is rubbish. The most appealing of all was a large painting by Frank Brangwyn, crowded with figures, superbly posed and coloured vividly but not garishly.

Following this introduction, I began to find out all I could about Brangwyn. I wasn't really surprised to learn that before the First World War, and up until the early 1930s, he was internationally famous, one critic describing him as 'the Rembrandt of tomorrow'. His work commanded high prices, reportedly the highest in the world until he was eclipsed by Picasso in the early 1930s. Beginning with realistic, precise paintings, his oils and watercolours then became, under the influence of the Impressionists, looser in style and with a more varied palette.

Through a number of large books written about him in his heyday, in quaintly hagiographic prose, I found that he also designed furniture, crockery, pottery, and windows for Louis Tiffany. His masterly compositions, ability to capture character and strong narrative sense led to commissions for huge murals, many of them in America. He never travelled to North America in all his long life, but his work is still to be seen there: notably in the Rockefeller Center, New York, and the Manitoba Legislative Building in Winnipeg. Perhaps the most striking is in the Herbst Theatre, San Francisco, where there are eight panels depicting the four seasons, each 7.6 metres high and 3.65 wide.

The high point of his career would appear to have been a commission from the House of Lords to paint the 'British Empire Panels'. This vast work, designed to fully occupy all four walls of the parliament's Royal Gallery, took seven years to complete. Brangwyn was shattered, although he made no public complaint, when it was rejected, in 1934, as 'too colourful and lively'. 'We must get used to these things in life,' Brangwyn said. 'Time alone will tell.' The murals can be viewed now in the Brangwyn Hall, Swansea—the artist's father was Welsh—and are perhaps the best reason for a visit to that city.

By the mid-1940s Brangwyn was a forgotten figure, a situation that has not really changed to this day, now that critical favour is firmly behind unmade beds (Tracey Emin), ossified animals (Damien Hirst) and scribbles (Cy Twombly). He retreated to the village of Ditchling, near Brighton, where he continued to paint almost every day, using the villagers as subjects. Among these was the actor Sir Donald Sinden, who told me, when I visited him in his Sydney hotel while he was on tour in Australia, that when he was eleven he and members of his family were models for some of the figures in the Rockefeller Center murals.

...

William Orpen was a small, feisty Irishman who studied in Dublin and then at the Slade School, London. (Brangwyn, in contrast, was self-taught, although his architect father was noted for his over-restoration, almost creation, of the Belgian city of Bruges.) Orpen's technical flair was apparent early in his career, and he painted everything from landscapes to mood pieces and character studies. He spent three years as a war artist, mostly in France, an experience that he found so disturbing he turned to drink, which hastened his death.

During the 1920s, however, he concentrated more and more on portraits, becoming the most eminent portrait painter in Britain and reputedly the highest priced in the world. His subjects were said to queue up in an annexe of his huge studio in Chelsea. Unlike Brangwyn (whose wife died in 1924—he never remarried), he lacked uxoriousness. He married in 1901 but subsequently had affairs with a number of his (female) portrait subjects, finally leaving his wife for one of them in 1912.

...

R. D. Elliott was born in Kyneton, Victoria, and left school aged twelve, which gave him an early start in business denied to his better-educated contemporaries. By the 1920s he owned a number of country newspapers, including Mildura's *Sunraysia Daily*. Opinionated and forceful, he was said to collect newspapers as they gave him an opportunity to expound his dogmatic views without being answered back.

He probably met Lord Beaverbrook while at a press conference in London in the 1930s and, through him, met Orpen (who painted his portrait) and, possibly, Brangwyn. His enthusiasm for their work, and his unbridled purchases, led his wife to refer to their Melbourne mansion as 'The Orpenage'.

By the time of his death, in 1950, the critical revolt against almost any kind of representational painting had reached its peak; the reputations of Brangwyn and Orpen had reached their nadir. Even by 1914, Brangwyn had been damned by Wyndham Lewis for his 'decadent irrelevance'. Both painters suffered from the mid-twentieth-century distrust of what I always considered to be their strength: an ability to draw, demonstrated in portraits and landscapes, bold compositions, vigorous and assured use of colour.

It is not surprising, therefore, that the National Gallery of Victoria in Melbourne, which was initially offered Elliott's collection of eighty-seven works by Brangwyn and forty-six by Orpen, refused the gift. Elliott's estate then turned to Mildura, where he had often holidayed on his houseboat.

. . .

The collection is remarkable and well worth the rigour of the journey. The Brangwyn collection is mostly of his superb drawings, which demonstrate both his insights into character (with his Ditchling neighbours as subjects) and his ability as a draftsman in his studies of buildings and—a lifelong obsession—bridges. There are also three superb large oil paintings, a number of charming watercolours, three vast murals and two large studies for murals—all of these typical of his work in their crowded compositions and bold colour.

The Orpen works in Mildura include the landscape, in oils, *Rocky Coast Scene at Howth* and the moody *The Tragedy* and *The Circus*, but the majority is a group of his accomplished portraits. As with so many artists, the most telling of these, with the most suggestion of the character of the sitter, are those of Orpen himself. He seems to be alive as he looks thoughtfully, questioningly, at the viewer, almost with a hint of anger at the intrusion into his private world.

A large oil of Orpen's, *Sowing New Seed* (now in Mildura), had created a scandal when it was originally bought by the Adelaide Gallery for the outrageous price of seven hundred pounds sterling. It shows a nude young woman, two nude children, and what appears to be a preacher and his wife. Orpen playfully offered various interpretations of its meaning, invariably contradictory. Many Adelaide citizens were outraged, although thousands of them forced themselves to visit the gallery to see the painting. Following complaints along the lines of the Reverend Sugden's that the picture was 'reeking with sexuality', it was eventually returned to London. Elliott bought it from Orpen in 1927 and returned it to Australia.

. . .

There are signs that the international reputations of both Brangwyn and Orpen may be making a comeback, just as the paintings of the recently neglected Lawrence Alma-Tadema, John William Waterhouse and Norman Lindsay have returned to favour. Orpen's work certainly reaches high prices in his native Ireland and I have found, in recent years, that my modest means now make it difficult for me to afford the Brangwyn drawings that find their way onto the market. My loss will be small indeed if these wonderful artists once again attain international recognition.

If the intrepid traveller has no interest in deserts, the Murray River, paddle steamers, vineyards, Brangwyn or Orpen, then there is one other reason to visit Mildura. The town boasts a restaurant, Stefano's, which is among the best in Australia.

. . .

In 2010 there was a retrospective of the work of Frank Brangwyn in Tokyo. Brangwyn has never lost popularity in Japan. In 2014 works by William Orpen featured in an exhibition of First World War paintings at the Imperial War Museum in London. And in Dublin a huge statue of Orpen by the sculptor Rowan Gillespie is to be placed in a public park before Christmas 2017.

2009

Caravaggio and the Cinema

There were plenty of painters of genius prior to Caravaggio (1571–1610)—El Greco, Bruegel, Michelangelo, Holbein, Bosch, Leonardo, Botticelli and Dürer, to name just a few—but I don't think it's too much of a generalisation to say that none of them had in such abundance the cinematic qualities, or factors, that Caravaggio brought to painting. These cinematic factors are composition, lighting and casting.

Those painters, no matter how great their talent, painted within a framework, a tradition. I suppose painters always do, at all periods of history. A lot of their commissions were from the Catholic Church and dealt with the lives of the saints, the Holy Family and various biblical stories. It was expected these were to be treated with reverence, so there are a large number of works in which various soulful types stare out at us. Portraits of members of aristocratic families may have been painted with realism, so that they emerged as recognisable individuals, but the vast majority of the biblical pictures were of idealised human beings.

Caravaggio had a different idea: he saw the characters in the Bible stories as human beings just like the rest of us. A contemporary of Caravaggio commented, 'when the most famous statues of Phidias were pointed out to him as models for his painting he had no other reply than to extend his hand to a crowd of men, indicating that nature had provided him sufficiently with teachers.' In his 1606 painting *Death of the Virgin*, for example, the virgin was reportedly modelled on a dead prostitute fished out of the Tiber. The church, not surprisingly, rejected the picture on the grounds it didn't comply with the decrees of the Council of Trent.

He had a great eye for the face that would make the painting come alive. His St Francis of Assisi and the boy who posed for St John the Baptist in the wilderness are full of character, passion, everyday life. Caravaggio knew how to cast a painting.

The Italian director Franco Zeffirelli spends as much time casting the extras in his films as he does the leading actors. He doesn't just throw in a bunch of people offered by Central Casting. Peter Jackson must have had the same approach with his outstanding *Lord of the Rings* trilogy, in which the faces of extras glimpsed for just a few seconds are arresting. It's just as easy to cast a film badly as it is to use bland models in a painting, something Caravaggio always avoided. (Even now, in London, directors have to use extras from a union, one with a surprisingly small membership, unless they're shooting more than thirty miles out of the city. This means the same boring—and bored—faces turn up in film after film.)

Caravaggio's compositions are fabulously cinematic. For a start, he practically invented the close-up. If he was going to use real people, to put real passions and real characters on the canvas, he must've decided that he might as well show them. Further, he knew that he'd heighten the effect if he used a plain background, so that the face is almost three-dimensional. This is a neat trick. If you look at the work of many of the great portrait photographers you'll notice that they've pinched Caravaggio's idea by shooting their subjects against a very simple background, as it's then quite difficult to produce an uninteresting image.

The great American film director John Ford I'm sure studied paintings, if not by Caravaggio, then by those he influenced. In a film like *Stagecoach* (1939), Ford shoots the close shots against a simple, uncluttered background, no matter what may be behind the actors in the wide shots.

He knew the shots would make a greater impact. It has been said that he had terrible eyesight and couldn't see the expressions on the actors' faces if the background was cluttered, but I think he studied Caravaggio—and other great painters.

Caravaggio's group compositions are equally startling. The figures are placed in a way that must've struck his contemporaries as wildly unconventional, not to say blasphemous. He seems to have had a wide-angle lens with which he arranged the figures in dramatic proximity. Any novice, or even accomplished, film director could do worse than study these compositions. In *The Conversion of Saint Paul* (1600–01), Paul isn't even facing us: he's fallen to the ground and could be in a drunken stupor instead of witnessing a miracle. The horse is seemingly about to tread on him and the ostler looks like the real thing, not some standardised biblical figure.

Further, and this is perhaps the most striking aspect of Caravaggio's paintings, there is the lighting. In painting after painting he chooses a single source which hits his subject sharply and throws dark shadows. This light usually appears to be a high window, somewhere up to the left of the subject, and it seems to me that he must've worked in a studio arranged for this purpose. This was a radical break with previous painters, whose lighting was almost invariably quite flat, no matter how brilliant their technique or how skilled their compositions. Contemporary critics of

Caravaggio complained that he was cheating—they weren't getting a fully painted picture because half of it was in darkness. It was even implied that he was too lazy to paint more figures, so just filled the canvas with black.

Caravaggio couldn't have cared much what they thought, because he went on painting in this style—the impact of which was enormous. He doesn't seem to have worried much what anyone thought about anything he did. He was a Bohemian before the Bohemians, and was accused of murder twice—once in an argument over a tennis-match wager. He finally came to an end at the age of thirty-nine on a beach in Sicily, where he either died from fever or was assassinated by the Knights of Malta. No one knows for sure. No one ever will.

His influence was vast. Caravaggism—the use of chiaroscuro, of light and shade—had many followers, among them Gentileschi, Rembrandt, Rubens, Velázquez, Vermeer, Poussin and so on.

When film began in the early years of the last century the lighting was invariably flat—just like the pre-Caravaggio painters. Attempts to introduce shadows were met with complaints from theatre owners who felt they weren't getting their money's worth if the screen was partially in darkness. The director D. W. Griffith overcame these objections by calling it 'Rembrandt' lighting: this seemed to silence the objectors.

I often find myself in galleries with cameramen before

starting a film and we spend a lot of time discussing composition and lighting. We study the classical masters; we don't bother too much with Jackson Pollock or Tracey Emin. The impressionists have had a huge influence on filmmakers. Just look at all those beautiful Australian period films.

Caravaggio and his school have clearly influenced film-noir thrillers. Orson Welles knew Caravaggio's work in detail, no matter how often he may have denied this. The stark photography and strong compositions of films like *Touch of Evil* (1958) and his extraordinary *Othello* (1951) bear this out in almost every shot and in their wild mood and florid emotions.

2004

Remembering B. S. Johnson

During the years I worked for the British Film Institute's Production Board a key part of my job was to meet the vast number of applicants for financial and technical assistance and, in effect, do a feasibility study of their projects, many of which were absurdly expensive or wildly impractical, or both. Those which seemed to be achievable were then presented to a committee chaired by Sir Michael Balcon, who had once headed MGM-British as well as founding Ealing Studios. A small number were selected for production, while those rejected frequently ran weeping to the press with cries of 'favouritism' and 'perfidy', and with numerous suggestions of bribery and skulduggery—otherwise, how could their obvious genius not have been recognised?

B. S. (Brian) Johnson was unusual among the applicants, as he was older than most and had already had two novels published, *Travelling People* (1963) and *Albert Angelo* (1964). He was a big man, rather overweight, with a huge head, bright blue eyes and a thick mop of blond hair. He had an engaging, direct manner. He quickly told me he knew nothing about making films but wanted to make a short from one of his poems, 'You're Human Like the Rest of Them', and wanted the editing to reflect the rhythm of the verse.

As the entire piece was to be set in a classroom, only one professional actor was needed—to play the teacher. Brian, who had taught in the East End (the setting for the engaging *Albert Angelo*), could easily find the boys necessary for a couple of days' filming. I worked out a budget, of only a few hundred pounds, and called up an Australian cameraman, David Muir, who I thought could photograph the film both stylishly and economically.

Sir Michael Balcon's committee approved 'You're Human…' without too much discussion. Brian's verse was earthy, vigorous and witty, appealing immediately to the highly literate group of assessors.

The filming of 'You're Human…' went smoothly. Brian knew exactly what he wanted from his class of boys and his lack of affectation removed any inhibitions they might have had. His insistence on cutting to the verse made the editing quite laborious, but it seems to have worked as Brian envisaged. The film was shown at a short-film festival at Tours, where it won the first prize, a beautiful bronze by Arp. I recall that some of the *Sight and Sound* staff were taken aback at the award. 'You mean,' one of them said to me in an incredulous tone, 'that those Production Board films are *good*!'

Brian and I stayed in touch through the late 1960s, before I returned to Australia in 1972. He was both gregarious and industrious. He wrote reviews for various magazines and turned out a series of critically acclaimed novels, which were perhaps overly influenced by Samuel Beckett. Brian was inclined to have holes printed in pages or insist on large areas of white space. One book, *The Unfortunates* (1969), had chapters that could be read in a random order. All unfortunate, in my view, as his strengths were his elegant prose and his observations of everyday life—his own everyday life. He believed that a genuine novelist wrote from his own experience and that the others were frauds. He even tortured himself by spending weeks on a fishing trawler in the North Sea for his wonderful novel *Trawl* (1966). His poems were similarly personal, one of the most startling being an examination of his own penis.

Depressed at the lack of sales of his works, Brian fought hard for authors to receive some payment from public libraries. The scheme was adopted but, of course, the public that didn't buy his novels didn't borrow them either.

I returned to London in 1973 for a screening of *The Adventures of Barry McKenzie*. Brian was characteristically effusive, assuring me that this rather inane comedy was but the beginning of a long directorial career. I was dubious.

Shortly after that, back in Sydney, my wife called me in my editing room to say that someone had phoned from London and that Brian Johnson had committed suicide. He had slashed his wrists in the bath and written on the wall, in his own blood, 'This is my last work.' My wife was in tears. I was devastated. Even after forty years I miss his warmth, his humour, his friendship. Lately, I've been rereading his novels and still regard him, as I did when I read them in the late 1960s, as a major twentieth-century writer.

2012

Madeleine and Me

In 1960 I was an indifferent student at Sydney University. In pursuit of the prettiest girls I joined the Sydney University Players, where I was an even more indifferent actor, easily outclassed by the stars of the era—who included John Bell, John Gaden, Germaine Greer, Arthur Dignam, Clive James and Robert Hughes.

Madeleine St John (she pronounced the name 'Synjin', though I understand her family preferred the standard 'Saint John') was to be found backstage, helping with the costumes and props. Definitely not one of the university's glamour girls, she still managed to be striking. Tiny and with rusty-red hair, she always reminded me of a sparrow with her darting movements, her beak-like nose, her inquisitive eyes. Her odd appearance contrived to prevent her performing in anything other than minor theatrical roles, although she was cast, rather mendaciously I thought, in a revue, *Dead Centre*, in which she appeared, singing, dancing and dressed in red crepe, as Lola Montez.

I can recall only a couple of conversations with her—all vague now (half a century later!)—including one where she expressed a passion for the poetry of Thomas Hardy. I distinctly remember being so in awe of her wide reading—'Are you really unaware of the work of Gwen Raverat and Djuna Barnes?'—her forthrightness and her wit, that, in order to prevent my self-esteem plummeting, I took evasive action. The factor which distinguished her from virtually all of our contemporaries was that she was the daughter of a famous father, Edward St John, a prominent QC and Liberal politician, though if father or family was mentioned she immediately made it clear the subject was taboo.

I left for England in 1963 and lost track of Madeleine for thirty years. My attempts at establishing myself as a film director slowly met with some success. One day, in 1993, I was having lunch with Clive James, by now an internationally known critic and poet, when he mentioned that a novel he'd just read, *The Women in Black*, was by our old university colleague Madeleine St John—and was a comic masterpiece. I bought a copy immediately, agreed with Clive's assessment and called the publisher for Madeleine's number.

She was cordial and cheery over the phone, said she'd seen a number of my films over the years and was delighted I wanted to film her novel.

A few days later I went to see her. She was living in a large apartment on the top floor of a council house building in Notting Hill. The area had been derelict but was now being gentrified. Madeleine must have qualified for rent assistance some years previously and there was no indication that her financial situation had improved. The furnishing was basic, the most striking items being a number of well-thumbed paperbacks and a vicious white cat, which snarled and clawed the air whenever it considered I had approached too close to its mistress.

She seemed to have become even smaller, the rusty-red hair maintained its aura with bottled assistance and she was almost permanently attached to an oxygen tank with a long tube—the result of emphysema. She was as sharp-tongued as ever and tartly dismissed my query about whether it was advisable to smoke so heavily with such a condition. She was happy to talk at length about literature, classical music and jazz. Her opinions, as always, were firm and precise—contemporary novelists being airily dismissed as a bunch of parvenus. Mitsuko Uchida, she insisted, was the finest classical pianist and Art Tatum the greatest jazz pianist.

Personal information was much harder to obtain, though I found out that she had married Chris Tillam, a fellow student from Sydney, in 1965. They had lived in San Francisco for a few years, where he studied film. Once his course was completed they decided to go to London. Madeleine went on ahead but 'he never arrived.' She made no further comments, so I gathered he had met another lady—and that was the end of the marriage.

She refused to discuss her Australian relatives, just as she had back at university, although she made vague references to their 'ill-treatment' of her. Subsequent meetings with a couple of charming members of her family, in Australia, have led me to believe that Madeleine never recovered, while still in high school, from the shock of the death, by suicide, of her mother. She then created a cast of evil relations who had accepted her father's remarriage.

In the late 1960s, following her alleged abandonment by her husband, she lived around London in a number of apartments, sharing with various Australian university friends. To the astonishment of some she fell under the influence of a dubious Indian mystic, Swami Ji, and for a couple of years adopted Indian clothes and assumed an Indian name.

She supported herself with odd jobs, mostly in bookshops and an antique shop in the West End, although she tried to vary this routine by applying, at one point, and unsuccessfully, for a position as Kenneth Tynan's secretary. It was not until sometime in 1991 that Madeleine decided to write a book herself, convinced, she told me, she could do at least as well as the authors of so many of the books she was selling.

She was fifty-two when *The Women in Black* was published in 1993 and it is the only one of her four novels to be set in Australia. It is difficult not to see Madeleine herself in the clever and sensitive young heroine, Lesley Miles, though the well-observed lower-middle-class family background she describes with such affection was certainly not her own, as she grew up in the smart suburb of Castlecrag, on Sydney's North Shore. It is probable that she appropriated the family of her university friend, Colleen Olliffe, who lived in a modest suburb. Colleen's father, like Mr Miles, was in the printing business but did not have the rather austere personality of Madeleine's father.

The novel was clearly set in a fictionalised version of the David Jones department store in Elizabeth Street, Sydney. The interplay of the saleswomen (who dressed in black in 1960, when the novel is set, just as they do now) is so convincing, so comprehensively realised, that I assumed Madeleine had a holiday job there while a student, but she insisted this was not the case, 'although I often went shopping there with my mother'.

Madeleine's subsequent novels, *A Pure Clear Light*, *The Essence of the Thing* (nominated for the Booker Prize) and

Stairway to Paradise, are, I think, equally superb—though none have the warmth and pervasive good humour of *The Women in Black*—and mark her as a major writer. The palette is small, but the observation and the dialogue acute, touching and often very funny. A fastidious stylist whose model was Jane Austen, she created, or recreated, a section of late-twentieth-century London society in a manner similar to Austen's world of the early nineteenth century. I remain astonished at the fidelity with which Madeleine captured the manners and mores of the middle-class English, as I was never aware that she knew many of these people. I assume that her years working in bookshops introduced them to her and her interpretive genius took over from there.

If Madeleine's social circle was not wide, there were a number of devoted friends who seemed to be able to cope with her changes of mood, her demands and general waspishness. Perhaps her fervent Christianity, acquired sometime after she dispensed with Swami Ji, supplied her with a moral code that meant she often found others wanting. At some point most friends and relatives were cast off.

A few managed a comeback but many, especially relatives, were in permanent outer darkness. Agents and publishers were almost saintly in the way they dealt with Madeleine's tantrums, her obsession with detail. She was aware, I realise, that a major strength of her writing was the accumulation of minutiae. She was so furious over some minor point in a French translation of one of her novels that she refused to allow it to appear. Kamikaze-like, she stipulated in her will that there were to be no translations of her novels into any language.

With a terrible sense of foreboding I sent her the screenplay of *The Women in Black*, written by Sue Milliken and myself. To my surprise, astonishment rather, she made no comment other than saying she looked forward to seeing the film. Perhaps she felt that if I could make a success of the intimate character studies of *Driving Miss Daisy* and *Tender Mercies* then I could do it again with her novel. It must have been a struggle, but she kept her reservations, and I can't believe they were not numerous, to herself.

Unlike so many of Madeleine's friends and associates I escaped being sent to Siberia—probably because I was only in London occasionally, was a link with university days (she enjoyed talking about our contemporaries) and shared Madeleine's interest in music. We even managed a visit to the Royal Albert Hall to hear Mitsuko Uchida play the Schumann Piano Concerto. Somehow, I engineered Madeleine down four flights of stairs in Notting Hill into a taxi, and then, complete with large oxygen cylinder, into a box near the stage.

On another occasion, I arranged to take her to dinner at the Ivy so that she could meet an American filmmaker she admired, Whit Stillman—the writer-director of three witty character-driven films dealing with middle-class Americans, *Metropolitan* (1990), *Barcelona* (1994) and *The*

Last Days of Disco (1998). Whit, a handsome young man, was polite but clearly bewildered by this tiny person with dyed red hair, an oxygen cylinder and forceful opinions. I also introduced her to my son, Adam, then a classics student at Balliol, and found myself somewhat bored as they discussed, at length, Adam's theory as to the identity of Shakespeare's Mr W. H. Madeleine assured Adam he had no idea what he was talking about.

Madeleine was always capable of surprising me. Her wild enthusiasm for the television series *Buffy, the Vampire Slayer* seemed to me totally out of character. I found a few episodes on DVD and failed, still fail, to see why this nonsense would have interested her. But then I have all of Willie Nelson's discs and my friends can't equate that with my passion for opera.

On one of my visits to London, a year or so before Madeleine died, there was no answer at the flat, so I feared the worst. Through her former literary agent, Sarah Lutyens, I tracked her down in a hospital on the King's Road. She was in a surprisingly stylish public ward with a television set suspended over the bed and numerous tubes connecting her to all sorts of sci-fi machines. Never one to complain about her unenviable health, she remained cheerful. She enjoyed meeting the other patients and nurses and hearing the stories of their lives.

She told me her blood count.

'Is that good?' I asked.

'My doctor says that for me it's very good,' she replied. 'If it was anyone else they'd be dead.'

That was the last time I saw her. We spoke on the phone a few more times, then an email arrived, in June 2006, saying she had died. She must have been bitterly disappointed that I had directed numerous other scripts but not *The Women in Black*, but had affected indifference. She also minimised the acclaim she had received for *The Essence of the Thing*, although it cannot fail to have meant a lot to her.

On her desk was a hundred pages or so of a new novel—a few typed but many in longhand and unnumbered. With the help of Sarah Lutyens the pages were arranged in their probable correct order. There are many characteristically witty and touching scenes, but the manuscript is too fragmentary for publication. Her will left her modest estate, as well as future royalties from her books, to charity. I was named her literary executor, in addition to which she left me a charming drawing, by Bernard Hesling, of the Sydney Conservatorium of Music. Various friends shared out her modest collection of books.

The angry cat was no problem, as it had predeceased her.

2009

A Remarkable Man

I first met Clive James in 1959. We were both students at Sydney University. I think he started there in 1958.

I saw Clive often over the next three years, although we were not great friends at this time. We were both indifferent actors, though I was the more indifferent, and came across each other occasionally during student productions, most of them dominated by students who went on to make a mark in Australian theatre—John Bell, Arthur Dignam and John Gaden. I still remember Clive's colourfully bizarre performance in *Lysistrata* and in annual university revues.

Clive was a celebrity on campus, while I was something of an awestruck lightweight. Clive wrote extensively for the university newspaper, *Honi Soit*. He contributed many poems, most of which I considered to be far superior to the work of other student poets, with the possible exception of Les Murray. Some of these appear in his recently published *Collected Poems: 1958–2015*, a work that I consider establishes him beyond question as a poet of the first rank.

Clive also wrote hilarious sketches for the university revue and could be found in one of the campus coffee shops at almost any time of day, surrounded by acolytes—a group that included many attractive girls—as he voiced his opinion on numerous subjects, with an emphasis on poets and novelists.

It was not difficult to be an intellectual lightweight at this time (though it's a role I feel I'm still playing), as the heavyweights were numerous and formidable. In the early 1960s they included Germaine Greer, Robert Hughes, Bob Ellis, Mungo MacCallum and Lawrence Nield.

I went to London in 1963 and bumped into Clive and Mike Newman, by chance, in Kensington High Street. Mike was also at Sydney University and had also contributed comic sketches to many of the revues. They were looking for someone to share a flat with them and, I think, rather reluctantly invited me to join them.

Despite Clive being an untidy and irresponsible flatmate he was invariably cheerful, witty and amiable. Over the next couple of years we became close friends, a friendship that has continued to this day. We went to numerous films and plays, concerts and poetry readings, art galleries and museums.

Clive's interests were astonishingly wide and his curiosity insatiable. I always found his opinions on virtually any subject, from literature to politics, economics, sport, *anything*—to be original, considered and well argued. His memory was, and is, incredible. A few years ago he and the poet Peter Porter had a BBC programme discussing poetry. I commented to Clive that the programme must have required a lot of preparation, as both he and Porter quoted extensively from a wide range of poets. Clive replied that they prepared nothing before the talks and the numerous quotes, often of entire poems, not just a line or two, were entirely from memory.

Clive's fascination with literature other than that written in English led him to master a number of languages, so that he could read the originals. He is fluent in German, French, Italian, Russian and Japanese. I'm not sure about his Greek and Latin, but have heard him talking on the phone in Czech—a language that even Czechs find difficult—though I'm not certain that Clive's grasp extends beyond a few polite phrases. I was astonished a couple of years ago to see him being interviewed in Japanese for a Japanese television programme.

...

Clive went up to Cambridge sometime in the late 1960s—around the time I returned to England after a couple of years in Nigeria. Again, he was a key writer for the university revue, Footlights, which led him into a career as a journalist. He also managed to appear in a television series, *Postcard from…*, write five brilliant volumes of autobiography, publish four or five novels, compose hundreds of songs (recorded by his old Cambridge friend Pete Atkin) and a huge amount of poetry, as well as complete an acclaimed translation of Dante.

After I returned to Australia in 1972 my career sputtered into life and I made, and am still making, films all over the world. This has meant Clive and I have seen less of each other but we have kept up a correspondence—at first by snail mail and now by email. And on my not infrequent trips to England I visit him in his Cambridge house. I remember how its tidiness amazed me the first time I saw it. His work desk is similarly free of clutter. He sits and writes for hours every day, using a pencil and an exercise book.

I am writing this short memoir in London in February 2017. I saw Clive just over a week ago. He is frail, with an unenviable host of maladies, but is as sharp intellectually as ever. Another two books (one of them a collection of new poems) are to be published within a few months.

A remarkable man. Perhaps the most remarkable I have ever met.

2017

Australian Literature and Film

A few articles have appeared in the press recently implying that Australian films would benefit if more adaptations were made from acclaimed literary works. Comparisons are inevitably made with foreign films, particularly English and American, where various eminent authors of those countries have had their works adapted to the screen.

Probably a majority of English-language films are adaptations of novels. Many of these would not be based on literary successes but, rather, popular fiction. But it isn't surprising, at least to me, that a number of writer-directors prefer to eschew adaptations and film their own original screenplays. Many are considerable artists and are reacting to the society in which they live. They prefer the comments, the attitudes, in the films to be their own and not a retread of some other writer's ideas, stories or characters. In the case of adaptations there is in any event usually little correlation between the standard of the original work and the film derived from it. *The Godfather* (1972) is one of the greatest of all American films but is adapted from a novel, by Mario Puzo, considered a potboiler.

It's worth pointing out that there is no intrinsic reason why literary film adaptations should be particularly successful, or why a high proportion of 'quality' novels should even be suitable for transcription to another medium. Many novels are famous for their prose style, various colourful characters, their themes and so on: factors which can obscure the fact that other useful ingredients—a coherent plot, for example—may be absent. In a film, most of the characteristics that distinguish a literary work—such as a striking prose style—are stripped away and this can reveal the lack of a well-constructed story, or convincing dialogue, and be fatal to the effectiveness of the film. Virtually all of the adaptations of Hemingway novels have been extraordinarily dull, while the delicate mood of F. Scott Fitzgerald's works have not been captured on screen, though the slight plotlines have been all too apparent. *The Great Gatsby*—so widely admired, such a fascinating novel—has been filmed five times, with results varying from 'disappointing' to 'disaster'.

Overall, England has fared well with adaptations of classic works, especially those of juicy and exuberant Victorian novels—often for television. Many of the Dickens, Thackeray and Trollope efforts have been quite outstanding, despite the film medium laying bare Dickens' quite inept plotting, with its reliance on coincidence for resolutions. Jane Austen, needless to say, has been a continued and resounding success. The BBC does a completely new version of *Pride and Prejudice* ever three or four years.

Twentieth-century English authors vis a vis film-makers have had mixed success. There have been acclaimed and quite delightful adaptations of E. M. Forster novels by the American director James Ivory. I particularly admire *A Room with a View*, *Howards End* (1992) and *Maurice* (1987), as well as *The Golden Bowl* (2000, from an incomprehensible novel by Henry James), but thought David Lean's much admired *A Passage to India* (1984) far less successful, as the essential ambiguity of the novel couldn't be transferred to images (at any rate not by David Lean), which are notoriously unambiguous. The satire and dry cynicism of Evelyn Waugh hasn't transferred well to film, either, apart from the television version of his one more or less conventional narrative, *Brideshead Revisited* (1981). The film of *A Handful of Dust* (1988), for example, never betrays the fact that it is adapted from one of the great comic novels. *Scoop*

(1987) and *The Loved One* (1965) bit the dust in a similar manner. Only Stephen Fry's frantic, lively *Bright Young Things* (2003), based on Waugh's *Vile Bodies*, captured the feeling of the original.

Looking through a list of the large number of Australian films made since the 1970s, it doesn't seem to me that Australian filmmakers have been ignoring the works of celebrated Australian authors.

Admittedly only one film has been made from a story by the most eminent (and I think the greatest) of all Australian writers, Patrick White: *The Night the Prowler*, scripted by White and directed by Jim Sharman in 1977. [Since I wrote this piece Fred Schepisi has directed a thoughtful adaptation of White's *The Eye of the Storm* (2011) with a high-octane cast including Geoffrey Rush, Charlotte Rampling and Judy Davis.] No other White adaptations have been attempted, partly because he may have been forgotten by most of the current generation of readers but most likely because his novels, like Conrad's, are psychological studies, intense and profound, and not easy to transfer to a film script. It's hard to imagine anyone trying to tackle the complexities of *Voss*, *Riders in the Chariot* or even the simpler *The Aunt's Story*. (Actually, I think White's first novel, *Happy Valley*, which has a more conventional narrative, could be successfully adapted to film.)

Apart from any other factors, the first two of these—his most acclaimed novels—would cost a fortune to make; they would require budgets generally well beyond local resources and on film would almost certainly lack the density of the books. They would likely appear to be nothing more than adventure stories dotted with odd characters. The various versions of Conrad—*Victory*, *Lord Jim*, *Nostromo*—lost all of their subtlety on screen, probably because it was impossible to find a way of capturing visually the essence of the novels. There was no equivalent way to describe Conrad's character insights. Only *The Duellists*, the Conrad novella adapted by Ridley Scott, seemed to me to have the atmosphere and mood of the original story.

Many years ago, I think in the late 1970s, the American director Joseph Losey (*The Servant*, 1963; *The Go-Between*, 1971) spent months in Australia preparing to film *Voss*. Somehow or other a copy of the script came my way. It read like an Australian western and could have been adapted from a novel by Jack Schaefer or Walter Van Tilburg Clark. The film of *Voss* was never made—I've no idea why, though the main reason films have a last-minute collapse is because all or some of the finance fails to materialise—and a disappointed Losey returned to his home in England.

...

Rather than try to build up intellectual credibility by tackling the metaphysics of authors like White, filmmakers are often better advised to adapt novels which rely primarily on a few strong characters and a compelling narrative. A strikingly successful example of this approach is Ted Kotcheff's 1971 film of Ken Cook's short novel *Wake in Fright*. The book won no literary prizes but its story of a schoolteacher in a ghastly outback town is well told, exciting and fast moving. Similarly, many of the novels of the prolific and unacclaimed (by the literary establishment) Bryce Courtenay have been made into both successful films and television miniseries.

The two living Australian writers who at the time of writing are the most eminent literary figures, not just in this country but worldwide, are Tim Winton and Peter Carey. Winton's novels strike me as bargain-basement Patrick White: stylistically derivative, they are far more savage, full of unpleasant characters and weakly plotted. This view, I should add, is not widely held. I've read a number of Winton novels in an effort to fall in line with so many of my friends and the international critics but have failed dismally. Two of his books have already been filmed—*That Eye, the Sky* (1994) and *In the Winter Dark* (1998). Neither was particularly successful, but the highly accomplished director Phillip Noyce has announced that he will be filming *The Riders*, and a film version of *Cloudstreet* has been announced as well. I hope it's a little more concise than the five-hour theatrical version of the novel. [*The Riders* had still not materialised in 2017 but a television miniseries of *Cloudstreet* was well received in 2011. It was directed by Matthew Saville from a script by Tim Winton and Ellen Fontana.]

Two of Peter Carey's novels have been filmed—*Bliss* (1985, directed by Ray Lawrence) and *Oscar and Lucinda* (1997, directed by Gillian Armstrong). Both were shown internationally and received critical raves.

Fred Schepisi made a powerful film (1978) of Thomas Keneally's *The Chant of Jimmie Blacksmith* and Peter Weir had a huge success with an adaptation (1982) of Christopher Koch's *The Year of Living Dangerously.* A delightful film (1983) was made by Carl Schultz of Sumner Locke Elliot's *Careful, He Might Hear You* and his *Water Under the Bridge* was made for television (1980). The one attempt at a Christina Stead (a turgid writer, in my worthless opinion), *For Love Alone* (1986, directed by Stephen Wallace), was not notably successful. I filmed Henry Handel Richardson's *The Getting of Wisdom* in 1977. Critics did not share my admiration for the result. Murray Bail's *Eucalyptus* was nearly filmed—with a cast that included Nicole Kidman and Russell Crowe—but it collapsed mysteriously a few days before shooting was due to begin.

These examples could go on but the point has been made, I think, that Australian filmmakers are certainly not unaware of Australian novelists. This issue is never as simple as saying, 'I want to make a film of such and such a book,' and then having it happen. Money is difficult to raise these days, as financiers want so many guarantees. Who is in the cast? Without a couple of guaranteed names it's almost impossible for any project to move forward. Are sales lined up around the world? It's very difficult to do this before the film is made, and often the name actors and director are not valued enough to ensure upfront finance.

A further problem is that admiration for and knowledge of a number of Australian classic novels is not necessarily widespread. Certainly the word of their excellence has not reached all of those in charge of making financial decisions. A few years ago I wrote an adaptation of Henry Handel Richardson's three-volume epic *The Fortunes of Richard Mahony*, from 1930. I didn't really expect potential investors to have read the novel (I wasn't even sure anyone but a few academics and myself had read it in the past half-century) but I did at least expect them to have heard of it—and her, the author. This was not the case. Clearly no one I spoke to in relation to finance had the faintest idea of what or who I was talking about. Not all that amazing these days. When preparing a film about Rachmaninoff, I found few investors/producers to whom his name meant anything; when I was planning a film about Mahler, a Hollywood studio executive said, 'What I can't understand is why you want to make a film about a nonentity.' I said nothing, but perhaps should have told him that one of the most gifted composers of all time could not accurately be described as a 'nonentity'—except by someone of overwhelming stupidity.

...

In 2017, more than ever, investors tend to consider their predominantly young audience wants nothing but action films, crude comedies, sequels and adaptations of comic strips. It has become harder to find the money to make more personal or more mature films. If they're financed at all, it's invariably with very low budgets. On the other hand, this has meant that in the past few years television productions have been aimed at a more sophisticated audience. American series such as House of Cards *and* Breaking Bad *have stunned the world. Perhaps there is still hope for a miniseries of* The Fortunes of Richard Mahony?

2007